To George Enteen and E. Nancy Markle
with gratitude

1st Edition Published 2015
by Onyx Neon Press

Cataloging data:
Import/Export: Thai English As Transnational Sexuality Studies /
Jillana Enteen.
1. Thailand, Bangkok 2. Gender and Sexuality Studies 3. Queer Theory
4. Sex Differences 5. Gender identity 6. Sex Differentiation
7. Transnational Sexuality Studies

ISBN 978-0-9854519-6-7

Cover Art & Design by Colleen Tully © 2015
(www.colleentully.com)

Typeset in Adobe Garamond Pro

Import/Export

Thai English As Transnational Sexuality Studies

by Jillana Enteen

Edited by

Chastity West | Jeffrey P. Martin

Table of Contents

Acknowledgments

I would like thank so many people for their help with the studies I conducted for this book, as well as the act of turning it from dissertation into publication. There are many people I'm leaving out because I've had innumerable exchanges over this manuscript in its many forms. The cast includes hundreds of strangers willing to talk with me, the great people interviewed in this collection, colleagues, friends, professors, and students of the many configurations of "Sexuality as Transnational" I have taught. I began this work with the generous funding from a Fulbright Research Grant to Thailand in 1995-1996 and have received incredible support through the book's publication, in 2015, at the hands of my amazing editor Jeffrey P. Martin, and copy editor Chastity West. I am greatly indebted to SPAN, the Sexualities Project at Northwestern. for their generous support in my finalizing this project and furthering my continuing research on Medical Tourism to Thailand. To cover designer and life-long friend, Colleen Tully. Colleen Tully and Cora Kaplan have offered support and suggestions from it's inception until it's publication. I have such gratitude for these beginners and finalizers and all the support they've provided.

In between, I owe so much to people who've been kind enough to participate in this study, many of whom are not named at their request, and many other people who have supported my work including Oat, Law, Pari Susan, Anjana Suvarnananda, Peter Jackson, Ara Wilson, Megan Sinnott, Varaporn Chamsanit, Nutsuppat Chantharin, Pat Yaojanuwat, and Nareumon Pratanwanich. My dissertation advisors Bruce Robbins, Abena Busia, Richard Miller, Louisa Schein, and Marc Manganaro, as well as guidance from Benedict Anderson, Cora Kaplan, Jonathan Goldberg, Cheryl Wall, and Ed Cohen, enabled me to write and think about this topic through the lens of cultural studies, and their support and intellectual engagement stays with me always.

I gratefully acknowledge friends, colleagues, and students who've been essential to this project including Lena Asfour (huge shout out!), Barrak Alzaid, Leah Barren, Héctor Carillo, Nutsuppat Chantharin, Aasim Chowdhry, Chris X. Franko, Wendy Gold, Steven Epstein, Kasey Evans, Zac Farley, Radhika Gajjala, Emily Gilbert, Jonathan Goldberg, E. Patrick Johnson, Michael J. Kramer, Vivian Kramer, Greg Lanier, Kesinee (Nongsau Fon), Sarah Lowe, Tori Marlan, Amy Partridge, Pornthep Prathanvanich, Evren Savci, Mary Weismantel, Michelle Wright, Albert Yan (also big thanks!), and Zoe Zolbrod. There are many more whom deserve my thanks.

Nothing could ever be more sustaining than my family, whom help in so many ways give me the time and space and support to study, learn, write, and be an odd academic: E. Nancy Markle, George Enteen, Sharon Enteen, and Doug Prusso are the best parents and siblings and supporters anyone could have. I extend my gratitude to my family—the 19 Mitzners on the bus including Isador, Marci, Billie, Melanie, Nicke, Bobby, Ginger, Mindy, Joe, and Kenzie—and the extended-Enteens, including Alice Enteen Learman, my goddaughter Ana-Nico Clèment, and my daughters Aaliya Rae and Marlena Fanon. Of course, I end with Askar, who has accompanied me during all my hours of revision.

Thank you, all.

Import/Export

Thai English As Transnational Sexuality Studies

by Jillana Enteen

1

Situating Bangkok: Globalization, Representations, and Specific Communities

The following pages trace the negotiations between imported and local conceptions of sexualities and genders that accompany Thailand's participation in international markets. Since English is the dominant language for the print, spoken, and computer-mediated communications that take place as a result of this participation, *Import/Export: Thai English As Transnational Sexuality Studies* examines the deployment of the English language to construct genders and sexualities in contemporary Thailand. The three communities I consider do not dismiss Thai cultural beliefs in favor of English-language imports; instead, the two, often disparate, discourses are incorporated and translated, expanding the numbers and types of representations generated by these communities. Furthermore, these negotiations with English-language assumptions about sexualities and genders are often exported from Thailand, adding new voices to international discussions.

While recent feminist and postcolonial works have revealed that inequities of power are embedded in transnational interactions, there have been few studies investigating the precise dynamics of these imbalances. Similarly, gender theories complicate notions of sexual and gender identities, but universalized assumptions of identity formation are often applied uncritically to non-western cultures. By considering, as editors Harper, McClintock, Munoz, and Rosen of *Social Text* 15.3/4 have suggested, "the interrelations of sexuality, race, and gender in a transnational context," I attempt "to bring the projects of queer, postcolonial, and critical race theories together" (1997, p. 1). These theories realign the way social experience is interpreted and de-center the voices previously privileged as those who generate truths. To address this cross-section of theories, I employ methodologies that cross disciplinary boundaries. In my analysis, I use textual analysis and close reading, ethnography, field research, archival work, and historical survey. In her influential Gender Studies/Queer Theory manuscript *Female Masculinities*, Judith Halberstam extends the term "queer" to denote her methodology: "I call this methodology 'queer' because it attempts to remain supple enough to respond to the various locations of information...and betrays a certain disloyalty to conventional disciplinary methods" (1998, p. 10). Similarly, the analyses in the following chapters exceed any single disciplinary method. By analyzing a broad range of what I consider "texts" culled from all resources available to me, I, too, invoke a "queer method." My exclusively English-language archive includes newspapers, magazines, government and non-government reports, fiction, websites, promotional and tourist videos, greeting cards, academic essays, historical accounts, and ethnographic texts such as events I attended and conversations and interviews that I conducted as a Fulbright Research Scholar. All of the data for this study was collected between August 1995 and June 1996 and in October 1996.

Opening their influential book, *Thailand's Boom!"* about Thailand's economic prosperity in the 80s and 90s, the pre-eminent team on Thai political and economic history, Phongpaichit Pasuk and Chris Baker argued "Understanding Thailand today means understanding the boom--where it came from, what it has done, where it is leading" (1997, p 1). Consequently, after reviewing the ways in which globalization has been invoked by cultural theorists, I situate the communities that I discuss by briefly describing the reasons for and ways in which Thailand experienced a decade of economic prosperity, highlighting the roles that the English language has played. After describing my methodology, I explain what I believe is at stake in the examination of representations. I then define two Thai concepts essential for understanding the ways in which contemporary Bangkok Thais envision themselves and others. Finally, I provide a summary of the following chapters.

The term globalization tends to be overused and vaguely

defined as an increasing transnational participation in an expanding late capitalist system. [1] Rather than attempting to account for the vicissitudes and contradictions of economic-based explanations and predictions, I employ a concise and useful definition provided by literary scholar, Gregory Jusdanus:

> Globalization signifies the transnationalization of capitalism, the breakdown of national economies, and the creation of a more interconnected world economic system. It also describes the emergence of new technologies of communication such as satellite, fax, and e-mail, which, along with the possibility of rapid intercontinental travel, alter the relationship between time and space. This spatial compression and temporal acceleration allow people, ideas, and goods to move with great speed, while also making it possible for individuals, however far apart, to witness events simultaneously. [2]

Jusdanus understands globalization to begin with economic interconnectedness, encompassing increased communication brought about by new technologies, rapid travel, and the simultaneous witnessing of events. In the process of globalization, social conditions and modes of consumption that cross national boundaries are linked to the travel of capital. In Bangkok, this would mean taking into account the increased

---

1   Like Mike Featherstone, discussed below, several writers in his edited collection, *Global Culture*, invoke globalization in a nonspecific way, assuming that it involves international market participation or increased communication among nations (1990).

2   Jusdanus, 1996, p. 141. See this essay for an overview of some of the definitions and assumptions by scholars and journalists..

availability and visibility of imported goods, technologies, ideas, and identities. But I must also emphasize that at this site, "things" that have traveled are no longer the same. The ideas, goods, and people that travel cannot retain the identical cultural connotations they once possessed because they exist in a new context, yet some of their social qualities still exist. Fredric Jameson, the cultural studies scholar renown for his articulate, specific descriptions of current labels and trends such as postmodernism and globalization, acknowledged the persistence of these social qualities by defining globalization of the late 20th century—as opposed to earlier globalizations he delineates for other notable factors-- as a "communicational concept, which alternately masks and transmits cultural or economic meanings" (1998, p. 55). Premising globalization on communication encourages the study of the way in which cultural and economic meanings shift in the process of travel. Communication, especially between cultures, is neither even nor transparent. Consequently, as Jameson has asserted, active economies with high volumes of imports and exports necessarily experience shifts in meanings.

Between 1986 and 1996, Thailand had one of the world's fastest growing economies, producing a high volume and variety of export products that generated a per capita income that increased exponentially. This growth affected every aspect of Thai society and most everyone in Thailand benefited materially: A substantial portion of the population was able to acquire electricity and a television set. For the first time, large numbers of Thai people sought employment outside their homes and social mobility. Reliable income entailed traveling from countryside towns and villages to Bangkok and often required working long hours with low wages. Prosperity had the largest impact on Bangkok natives, creating a new middle class and opportunities for education, employment, and the purchase of both domestic and foreign luxury items for both men and women.

The economic boom was instigated by the revaluation of the Japanese Yen in 1984. Because of Japan's huge trade surplus, many Japanese firms looked elsewhere to manufacture. The Thai government provided an atmosphere with few regulations, a liberal trade policy and almost no import duties (Mardon & Paik, 1992, p. 161). In addition, foreign, and local banks could take deposits and lend in foreign or domestic currencies, both in Thailand and abroad. The Thai currency was pegged to a "basket of currencies" of which the US dollar made up over 80 percent. Not only was the currency fixed to foreign investment, "Between 1986 and 1993, Japanese firms invested US $47 billion in Asia," and other Asian countries with strong economies followed suit (Pasuk & Baker, 1997, p. 3). During this decade, local Thai firms also increased their export-oriented manufacturing and the number and types of products assembled quickly grew. Bangkok's population surged, doubling during this decade, and residents prospered. The local marketplace became increasingly international, with imported European cars and other western luxury items available and esteemed. [3]

---

3   For a thorough account of the economic and cultural changes in Thailand during this decade, see Pasuk Phongpaichit and Chris Baker's *Thailand: Economy and Politics* (1995) and *Thailand's Boom!* (1996). Since the time of my research, the Thai economy has taken a drastic turn for the worse. The Baht, Thailand's monetary unit, was no longer valued according to a "basket" of currencies, the largest of which was the US dollar. Floating freely in international

Prosperity had the largest impact on Bangkok residents, creating a burgeoning middle class. The new middle class is made up of college-educated people with uncensored access to the Internet, imported media, and other international tourists/business people.[4] As a result, they possess an increasingly international outlook that is reflected in their tastes and consumption. Mobile phones, western-made cars, and western name brand clothing are possessions *de rigueur* for Bangkok professionals. Not only are western products consumed, but so are "ideas, ideologies and politics" from outside of Thailand (Pasuk & Baker, 1997, p. 409). However, while some practices and expectations changed to reflect increasing prosperity and exposure, many of Thailand's traditional societal values remained intact.

English-language accounts of Thailand's economic boom consistently comment on the inclusion of foreign ideas and practices. As Pasuk and Baker have described, since 1987 Thailand, especially Bangkok, has flourished in terms of economic development and the circulation of ideas. The economic boom has been accompanied by an increased openness to foreign ideas and products throughout the population.[5]

currency markets resulted in a drastic, unforeseen devaluation. As a result, an I.M.F. bailout began in December 1997.

4   I am not asserting that these media are not each without its agenda that affects the way in which the information is presented. For example, sites on the Internet exist in order to create desires for consumption, form certain types of international gay communities, create women centered and/or feminist communities, change political policies, and/or initiate friendships.

5   One interesting result is the popularity of *luk krung* (biracial Thais, literally "half children"). A large number of singers and actors in Thailand's prolific music, television, and movie industries are of mixed race, and a significant number of them have been raised outside of Thailand. This marks a huge ideological shift—*luk krung* used to be vociferously rejected by Thai society because they symbolized a woman's involvement with a westerner, which alluded to prostitution. Until the end of the twentieth century, *luk krung* were ineligible

Initially, Thai leaders and citizens as well as multinational banks and businesses viewed this openness with optimism. In his introduction to *Gender and Power in Affluent Asia,* internationally recognized media scholar Krishna Sen has explained, "The phenomenal rise of East and Southeast Asian economic power was frequently presented as the panacea for the ills of the West and East alike" (Sen, 1998, p. xi). However, inherent inequities may accompany these imports. Professor Sen continued, "But the picture always appeared a little cloudier to those of us who saw the process as a gendered one and who did not want to forget that citizens everywhere—even in a period of 9 percent growth—remain divided by class and sex" (Sen, 1995, p. xi). Gender and class discrimination, such as increasing inequalities between educated and labored workers, are some of the western practices that accompanied the boom.

Almost all communication between Thais and non-Thais in Bangkok takes place in English. It is the primary language both for conducting international business and for forming informal liaisons with *farang* (westerners). Thus communicating in English is perceived by Bangkok Thais as an essential component of securing financial success. In the first English language study of non-normative sexualities in Thailand, *Dear Uncle Go,* Peter Jackson and Eric Allyn have further elucidated the perception of English, "English has an exotic and cultured sense for many Thais, having associations with wealth, education, culture, modernity, and sexual liberality" (Jackson, 1995, p. 236). Many Bangkok Thais, especially the young middle class, associate English use with prosperity, the influx of daring new ideas, and an increased number

---

for Thai citizenship and were not entitled to government mandated education or health care afforded to non-Thai citizens with government issued work permits.

of ways to articulate sexualities and genders. Because English functions as a second language, it can provide a sense of freedom. Well-known French actor Lambert Wilson explained in an interview that playing English-speaking roles in American films such as the Matrix Reloaded language is easier than acting in his native tongue: "I feel it protects me. It works like a light mask so I can be a little less inhibited. It's also an easier language to act in because it's more flexible, it's more elastic" (Riding, 1998, p. 18). In the following chapters, English is repeatedly described by members of the communities that I study as providing economic privilege, reflecting modern culture, allowing for international dialogue, and enabling articulations inappropriate or more difficult to voice in Thai.

The invocation and adaptation of English by Thais differs according to each community I survey. On this note French political philosopher Etienne Balibar has written, "It is always possible to appropriate several languages and to turn oneself into a different kind of bearer of discourse and of the transformations of language" (1992, p. 98). "Bearing" English enables Thais to transform it meaningfully for themselves. Consequently, every time a Thai "bears" an English-language concept, it transforms to reflect the speaker and the context. Rather than presuming English as a global/universal language, Semiotics Professor Walter Mignolo argued, "when a Korean businessman and a Chinese banker speak in English they are not carrying in that conversation the weight of English/American civilization" (1998, p. 41). Mignolo explained further, "In the domain of literature, for instance, one can write in English and still add to it the density of Spanish/Latin American memories, as Latino/as are doing in this country" (1998, p. 41). Importing English does not lead to uncritical absorption. Instead, exported ideas change the language through its adopted use. This kind of assimilation and adaptation is evident, for example, in the way self-identified gay Thai men consider the term "gay" (Chapter Two), in the resistance of Bangkok women-who-love-women to English-language terms denoting their sexualities (Chapter Three), and in the use of romanticized images of Thai women by Thai women-centered Non-Government Organizations (NGOs) to garner international support (Chapter Four).

Thus the process of globalization, premised on economic activity and the participation in international markets, necessarily entails complicated modes of communication. As the dominant language of globalization, English functions to articulate these discussions and imported ideas. The arrival of English-language products, terms, and ideas includes notions of genders and sexualities. How these are incorporated, resisted, and adapted in Bangkok will be explored in the upcoming chapters. First, however, I will explain where I situate my examination.

Localized Study

Arjun Appadurai, a celebrated anthropologist of modernity and postcolonial theory who has been credited with decentering western assumptions, asserted, "The new global cultural economy has to be seen as a complex, overlapping, disjunctive order that cannot any longer be understood in terms of existing center-periphery models."[6] He has proposed that the relationship between five terms, or "landscapes," that he has created establishes a framework for looking at "these global cultural flows" (Appadurai, 1997, p. 33). While these landscapes do serve to clarify some of the ways in which cultures are currently intersecting, the examples he gives to necessitate their implementation rely on simplistic generalizations. The instance most relevant here is, "These tragedies of displacement could certainly be replayed in a more detailed analysis of the relations between the Japanese and German sex tours to Thailand and the tragedies of the sex trade in Bangkok" (Appadurai, 1997, p. 39). While he calls for a more detailed analysis, he does not provide one and never again mentions the sex trade in Bangkok in his book-length study. Yet this is not a mere observation: the deployment of the word "tragedies" implies an already established conclusion, the victims of which are, by and large, the bodies of Thai women. That Appadurai, a celebrated postcolonial theorist credited with decentering western assumptions, maps the global cultural flows of the Thai nation onto the Thai sex-trade and, by extension, Thai women as sex-workers illustrates two important points—that the application of postcolonial theory may perpetuate rather than dismantle discrimination, and that these stereotypes about the predominance of the sex-trade and the participation by Thai women remain deeply embedded in non-Thai

---

6   p. 32. Appadurai's eagerly anticipated book *Modernity at Large* (1996) does not push past anecdotal evidence, nor does it display the rigorous analysis he called for in his 1990 essay "Disjuncture and Difference in the Global Cultural Economy." Instead, much of the book consolidates earlier essays. A version of the essay that does not rise to his own challenge appears as the foundation for his second chapter.

considerations, continually informing analysis and critique. This study reveals sites where these assumptions go unnoted and examines their effects on the presentations made by Thai people entering into English-language discourses about genders and sexualities.

Anne McClintock has suggested in *Imperial Leather* that postcolonial theory may be unable to dismantle discriminatory western practices:

> If postcolonial *theory* has sought to challenge the grand march of Western historicism and its entourage of binaries (self-other, metropolis-colony, center- periphery, etc.), the *term* postcolonialism nonetheless reorients the globe once more around a single, binary opposition: colonial-postcolonial. Moreover, theory is thereby shifted from the binary axis of *power* (colonizer-colonized itself inadequately nuanced, as in the case of women) to the binary axis of *time*, an axis even less productive of political nuance because it does not distinguish between the beneficiaries of colonialism (the ex-colonizers) and the casualties of colonialism (the ex-colonized). (1995, p. 11)

McClintock worries that the term postcolonial re-centers considerations on the ex- colonizer's axis of time. Applying a western theory based on the experience of colonialism indiscriminately on countries with different colonial circumstances can only lead to false or overgeneralized conclusions. Post-colonial theorist Rey Chow has asked, importantly, of the subfield she finds her positioned, "Is the 'post' in 'postcolonial' simply a matter of chronological time, or does it not include a notion of time that is not linear but constant, marked by events that may be technically finished but that can be fully understood only with consideration of the devastation they left behind?" (1998, p. 151). Appadurai assumed the former, situating the world in a postcolonial moment without acknowledging that histories inform present day circumstances, actions, and interpretations. Concern about the validity of conclusions drawn from the lens of postcolonial theory is especially relevant when considering countries that have never been colonized or countries that, like Thailand, have experienced colonial pressure without sacrificing their independence.[7] Discussions of the postcolonial condition must therefore take into account Thailand's specific circumstances. Extending not only postcolonial theories but also incorporating multiple theoretical perspectives that consider radically shifting inequities through lenses of Thai studies, queer theory, gender theory, and cultural studies will better enable the following study to render more visible the complex intersections, the politics of oppression and struggle, and the relationships between center and periphery, Western vis-à-vis the global south, Thai, and these Thai subcultures in particular. I hope to breakdown rather than stimulate further economic and cultural inequities and reveal some of the knowledge production done by these spatially and temporally

---

7　The British, French, and American governments pressured Thailand. Britain considered taking over Thailand when it colonized Burma, but the Thai king was able to present Thailand, Thai culture, and the Thai people in terms understood and appreciated by the British colonizers, enabling Thailand to remain unoccupied. See Winichakul's *Siam Mapped* for an excellent account and analysis, parts of which I summarize in my third chapter (1994). During the Vietnam War, U.S. troops were based in Northern Thailand and the beach area south of Bangkok served as the premiere rest and relaxation (R'n'R) site for American troops stationed in Southeast Asia (1994, p. 12).

situated groups as it is in dialogue with these prominent academic, often western derived, discourses.

By following the strategy of historians George Chauncey and Richard Cornwall, who connect class and economics to sexuality in the United States at the turn of the twentieth century, I will show that the process of globalization bonds sexualities and conceptions of gender with economies, and by centering the local I can delineate how non-indigenous sexualities and western notions of gender coexist, interact, and adapt in Thailand. [8] In the past decade feminist, sex, and gender theories have addressed the erasure of specific bodies in terms of race and class of individuals located in the west.[9] Even more recently, work has begun that extends this theorizing beyond western culture and location and re-theorizes according to localized situations.[10] Hence the notion of sexual identity is being complicated, but universalized assumptions of identity formation are still frequently applied unproblematically to non-

---

8   See Chauncey for an excellent historicizing of sexual identity as well as an extensive discussion of the links between sexuality, class, and economics (1994).

9   See Cheryl Wall's collection, *Changing Our Own Words* (1991); Abena Busia and Stanlie James' *Theorizing Black Feminisms* (1993); Gayatri Spivak's *In Other Worlds* (1993) and *Outside in the Teaching Machine* (1998); and sections of Judith Butler's *Bodies that Matter* (1993). The following collections discuss the necessity for site specificity in terms of how feminism should be constituted, but spend little time exploring the specific nature of sex, gender, and sexualities: the collection *This Bridge Called My Back* edited by Cherrie Moraga and Gloria Anzaldua (1981); *Feminist Genealogies, Colonial Legacies* edited by Chandra Mohanty and M. J. Alexander (1996); *Third World Women and the Politics of Feminism,* edited Chandra Talpade Mohanty, Ann Russo and Lourdes Torres (1991); and Kumari Jayawardena's *Feminism and Nationalism in the Third World* (1986).

10   See, for example, Herdt's edited collection *Third Sex, Third Gender* (1994); Martin F. Manalanson IV, "(Dis)Orienting the Body: Locating Symbolic Resistance among Filipino Gay Men" (1994); and Ana Maria Alonso and Maria Teresa Koreck, "Silences: 'Hispanics,' AIDS, and Sexual Practices" (1993).

western cultures. As Dennis Altman has explained, almost ironically in the opening to *Global Sex* (2001), the first book dedicated to the topic: "It has become fashionable to point to the emergence of 'the global gay,' the apparent internationalization of a certain form of social and cultural identity based on homosexuality" (2001, p. 17). While this "global gay" image is being produced by both the west and the east and its embodiment can be seen in the gay locales in Bangkok, the international gay male is a fictive construction that has no literal embodiment, nor is it manifest in all social, political, and cultural contexts.

The majority of western sex and gender theory uses Foucaultian methodology to explain sexual identity as a cultural production or result of social forces.[11] Congruously, theorists in the field of sex and gender have argued that the notion of sexual identity is historically distinct, emerging as a result of the adoption of individualism. The notion of an individual body discrete from its history and community prefigures this body's articulation of its individuality through the internalization of identities. For example, economist Richard Cornwall has tied individualism to the market system:

> This ideology of the total separateness of each "rational" individual, able to choose independently and freely, splendidly isolated by her/his libertarian shield of property rights, arose along with the sanctity of property rights in the sixteenth and seventeenth centuries... This

---

11 This methodology is laid out in Foucault's *The History of Sexuality* (1980). Many other academics write about the social construction of sexuality and gender from psychoanalytic and Marxist perspectives. Judith Butler has also been influential in defining sexual identity through performativity (1990 and 1993).

bourgeois sense of individualism was both born by and
gave birth to the market-system, and has implied a respect,
by the individual, of the property/body/privacy of others.
(1997, p. 107)

By marking the moment where individualism becomes an assumed right,
and thereafter assimilated as "natural" by members of the community,
and linking this moment to the emergence of a specific type of
economics, Cornwall explained individualism's emergence and critiques
its naturalness. Since Thailand does not share this history, its sexuality has
emerged differently. Dominant Thai cultural discourses did not privilege
a bourgeois sense of individualism, nor did the country participate in the
same experience of colonizing or colonization that western countries and
those countries that they exploited experienced.[12] Rather than mapping
western histories and theories unproblematically onto Thai bodies,
new explanations based on the situations in Thailand must be devised.
Scholars publishing on Thai gender and sexuality such as Peter Jackson
(1993, 1999, 2011), Rosalind Morris (1994), Thook Thook Thongthiraj
(1994), Ara Wilson (2004) and Megan Sinnott (2004) have reevaluated
the usefulness of using western theories of identification to describe Thai
notions of sexuality. They looked specifically at Thai history and charted
changing representations of sexualities in response to cultural events.

Few studies look at specific market occurrences and their effects

---

12 This is not to say that Thailand has not colonized in any sense of the
word. The hill tribes in northern Thailand, for example, still simultaneously suffer
and benefit from attempts by the Thai government to alternately include, assim-
ilate, alter, and/or reject their cultures and attempts at maintaining, or in some
cases changing, their lifestyles.

on local cultures.[13] For example, most of the essays in a 1996 collection about globalization and its effect on culture entitled *Global Modernities* examine the types of theories being generated, not the way in which changing markets affect specific cultures.[14] Economic anthropologist Saskia Sassen proposed that those "othered" by the dominant powers of globalized economies still exist; they are just devalued. Consequently, these "non-dominant peoples and cultures" (Sassen, 1996, p. 180) can be centered. She argued: "understanding [this otherness] as a set of processes whereby global elements are *localized*, international labor markets are constituted, and cultures from all over the world are de- and re-territorialized, puts them right there at the center along with the internationalization of capital as a fundamental aspect of globalization" (Sassen, 1996, p. 190). Localized examinations of the representations produced by non-dominant peoples and cultures will provide this centering.[15]

---

13 An exception to this tendency can be found in Dennis Altman's "Global Gaze/Global Gays" (1997) and Saskia Sassen's "Analytic Borderlands: Race, Gender, and Representation in the New City" (1996).

14 *Global Modernities*. Ed. Mike Featherstone, Scott Lash and Roland Robertson (1990). In this volume, essays such as Roland Robertson's "Glocalization: Time-Space and Homogeneity-Heterogeneity" (1995) categorize the type of theorists and theories about globalization. None of these essays focus on a specific site.

15 In dealing with centering these local populations from a spatial and temporal distance, I have chosen to vary my terms for general areas or currents of thoughts throughout the pages which follow, so as to keep "globalization" in a dynamic context and remaining aware of local positionings. At times when I refer to Thai culture, I am referring to what a specific interview subject or scholar has deemed general. I use terms like the west to mean a means for constructing and situating knowledges, as well as to denote origins in the United States or Europe. I purposely counter the west to Thailand—uneven yet useful based on the scope and focus of this study, and I also switch popular vocabularies for dividing and categorizing economies. I refer to Thailand sometimes as the third world--implying a first and second world was already a misnomer when the

Examining Representations

The connotations of the word "representation," post-colonial feminist scholar Ella Shohat has explained, "are at once religious, aesthetic, political and semiotic" (1995, p. 166). Extensive debates have taken place about issues of representation and voice, as well as questions about whether actual subjects or cultural constructions are at stake. Shohat and her contemporaries revisited this contested terrain in feminist and postcolonial discussions of the late 1990s. In the crucial reevaluation of women and nation contained in *Real and Imagined Women*, Rajeswari Sunder Rajan revealed the "mediating function" of representation: "the concept of 'representation,' it seems, is useful precisely because and to the extent that it can serve a mediating function between the two positions, neither foundationalist (privileging 'reality') nor superstructural (privileging 'culture'), not denying the category of the real, or essentializing it as some pregiven metaphysical ground for representation" (1993, pp. 9-10). This is the reason why feminist scholars have found representation such an important concept in relation to the position of women in cultural contexts; representation

---

terms were circulating in the 1960s, 70s, and 80s as a result of cold war politics. I locate Bangkok and Thailand, at points, as part of Southeast Asia, and at others, as part of the ASEAN community. Term switching will the idea that any groups or studies can be monolithically, timelessly situated. The idea of the positioning of Thailand shifts often—as I write this "Amazing Thailand" has been placed on the US travel warnings list because of political unrest). I will not refer to Thailand as a developing country, however. While the positioning of Thailand may read, at times, awkwardly, I hope that it keeps the language use I am discussing in a constantly shifting, locally acknowledged, discursive space.

is a domain carrying substantial political effects. Our understanding of the problems of "real" women cannot lie outside the "imagined" constructs in and through which "women" emerge as subjects. Rajan's negotiation between the "foundationalist (privileging 'reality')" and the "superstructural (privileging 'culture')" usefully privileges neither. Representation as this neither/nor, insinuating both affective and material effects is a premise upon which I contextualize the following groups I examine. I consider the sexed and gendered representations of these Thai communities as well as the strategies employed by those who represent themselves and others in terms of sex and gender to be located at this unstable juncture. This understanding of representation acknowledges, for instance, that Thai women neither conform to nor exist outside of the general categories of sex-worker and/or wife that circulate on the Internet, nor are they embodied or misrepresented by the production of romanticized images as weavers or industrial manufacturers deployed by Thai women-centered NGOs. Instead, Thai women are in dialogue with the representations that they generate and those produced about them. They are affected by these images, but can, in turn, affect their production, circulation, and acceptance.

Representations about members of a particular nation affect the way in which that nation is understood. Consequently, representations of Thai women such as those that depict them as either sex-workers or wives extend, coloring the image of the Thai nation. Anne McClintock's assertion about nationalism, "All nationalisms are gendered, all are invented and all are dangerous" (*Imperial Leather*, 1995, p. 352), is also applicable to national representations. Since national image is invented as well as gendered, examining gender is essential for understanding national representations. Rajan has explained why these representations must be critiqued:

> If we acknowledge (a) that femaleness is constructed, (b) that the terms of such construction are to be sought in dominant modes of ideology (patriarchy, colonialism, capitalism), and (c) that therefore what is at stake is the investments of desire and the politics of control that representation both signifies and serves, then the task of the feminist critic becomes what Jacqueline Rose describes as "the critique of male discourse" born of "a radical distrust of representation which allies itself with a semiotic critique of the sign."[16]

Only by examining the way in which "femaleness is constructed" can we uncover the "investments of desire and the politics of control" embedded in national representations. [17] Accordingly, this study assumes that the presentations of Thai genders in national representations affect the ways in which the nation and its members construct and understand

---

16 1995, p. 129. Quote from Jacqueline Rose comes from "The State of the Subject (1): The Institution of Feminism" (1987, p. 11).

17 There are many collections containing excellent examinations of the gendered aspects of national discourses that are generated within nations and in colonial accounts. See *Nationalisms and Sexualities* edited by Andrew Parker, Mary Russo, Doris Sommer and Patricia Yaeger (1992); *Women, Ethnicity, and Nationalism* edited by Rick Wilford and Robert L. Miller (1998); *Writing Women and Space* edited by Alison Blunt and Gillian Rose (1994); *Space and Place: Theories of Identity and Location* edited by Erica Carter, et al (!993); *Place and the Politics of Identity* edited by Michael Keith and Steve Pile (1993); and *Space, Place, and Gender* by Doreen Massey (1994)..

themselves, as well as the ways in which they are produced and perceived by non-Thais.

In conclusion, in order to examine the specific effects of globalization, I link economic exchanges to those of uneven communication in English, the dominant language of the late capitalist market system. Analysis of representations, which include oral, visual, and written texts generated by the three communities I study, allows me to mediate between what Rajan terms reality and culture, acknowledging the influence of both. By historicizing my study and examining many sources, I neither assume that western productions of gendered and sexual identities apply to Bangkok Thais, nor do I ignore the presence of these constructions and the potential they possess for changing previous conceptions. In order to situate these communities, two Thai notions are central to understanding their position. They are defined below.

Farang

Instead of employing western words to note the westerners and western ideas present in contemporary Bangkok, I will use the Thai word *farang* (as a noun, both singular and plural and as an adjective), which is derived from "francais" in French. Adapting the word to suit their intent—a frequent Thai practice—Thais altered the original meaning extending it to designate most non-Asians, especially Europeans and Americans, in Thailand. Thais have specific words to denote the race or ethnicity of other Asians—Chinese, Japanese, Koreans, and Laotians. South Asians who have lived in Thailand for several centuries and have acted as trading partners and visitors with Thailand as long as Thai recorded history (including, significantly, the origins of the belief systems from which Theraveda Buddhism, Thailand's national form of Buddhist practices), are referred to as *khon khek*, or guests. The word *farang* is ubiquitous in Bangkok and throughout Thailand, and is well known by westerners that stay in Thailand for more than a couple of days. Thais use the word to refer to a person when speaking Thai if the non-Thai name is uncommon. I will use this term rather than a non-Thai word to describe non-Asians in Bangkok since it affects how these groups of people are imagined by Thais and by themselves in Thailand. The word *farang* reflects how Thais conceptualize the recent (last 300 years) groups of peoples who have appeared in Thailand and pressed or positioned their economies and cultures with those of Thailand.

In a similar manner, I have used many terms to designate the position of Thailand vis-à-vis Western Europe and North America. Since 2010, Western Europe and North America has been designated WENA as opposed to situating this area as the west and designating other areas the non-west. Rather than reflecting the contemporary political practices, however, I have chosen to use words to position Thailand that were those used during the time and place when I conducted these studies. Thus for each the groups of Thais I discuss in the following chapters, I use the language they use when speaking of Thailand and the rest of the world. Consequently, some sections will talk about western ideas, without differentiation to where these ideas emerged. At other points, I use terms such as "Asian" to designate the countries that might, post 2000, designate themselves as members of ASEAN. Developed, developing, and non-developed are terms for nation-states and their economies that I scrutinize in Chapter 4, and 3rd World and the Global South appear at moments in this book when the people I'm discussing have used these terms.

Thai-ness

The simplicity of the description of Thai identity belies the often-conflicted obligations it requires. "Thai-ness" is the term employed to denote what it means to be Thai. Thai-ness has many attributes, but Thai interconnectedness to family, society, Buddhism, the king (who is considered inextricably linked to Thereveda Buddhism), and each other as "Thai people," is consistently promoted as a crucial aspect of Thai-ness. Membership and commitment to these intersecting groups, not the sense that one is an individual possessing certain rights and freedoms, is recounted for *farang* in introductions to Thailand from many sources—guidebooks, cultural introductions to Thailand, [18] and material developed by the Tourism Authority of Thailand (TAT). While Thai-ness is inherent to Thai people through their family and education, it is in some sense untranslatable, and thus is subject of a cottage industry of constantly

18 See Denis Segaller, *Thai Ways* (1993), William J. Klausner, *Reflections on Thai Culture* (1993), Robert, and Nanthapa Cooper, *Culture Shock! Thailand* (1990). There are many books of this ilk that explore the complexity of Thai-ness. For instance, *Very Thai: Everyday Popular Culture* by Cornwel-Smith and Goss (2004) sold out and was revised and expanded as *Very Thai: Everyday Popular Culture 2* in 2013. Books about Thai-ness are constantly coming out in English and Thai English language bookstores normally have at least ten different books available as what seems so concrete to Thais sustains the publications of numerous explanations.

changing English-langue books printed by Thai presses. In the TAT's *Thailand in the 90s,* this interconnectedness is described through the family unit:

> Perhaps the best way to comprehend Thai social values is to focus on its basic unit, the family, and in particular the rural family in its typical village setting. Generally this will be an extended family. ... Respect for elders is taught very early, ... and by the time a child walks he is aware of his position in the family hierarchy, a distinction that applies not only to the relationship between parents and children but also to that between siblings of different ages. This same delineation of roles also applies to the wider world outside the family and will remain deeply ingrained throughout life (1995, pp. 56-57).

As recounted above, Thai children see themselves as part of their extended family, community, and nation from a very early age, and with this participation comes the willing acceptance of responsibilities and obligations.

While this feeling of commitment and interconnectedness begins at the level of family, it extends past the family and incorporates religion and nationalism. Being Thai is a developed, explained, and promoted identity in Thailand. Thai Studies Anthropologist Rosalind Morris (1994, 1997) has written, "Since Chulalongkorn's reign (1868-1910), national education has provided the means by which students are interpellated as Thai subjects and instilled with the moral values by which each of them can be adjudicated in relation to ideal Thai-ness (khwaam-pen-thai)" ("Educating Desire" 1997, p. 55). For example, the first textbook that all children throughout Thailand receive after they learn their alphabet and the basics of reading is called *Chiwit Nai Chat* (*Life in the Nation* [translation mine]). The text starts with an explanation of the symbols of the Thai flag, then describes members of the Royal Family past and present, explicitly directing students to show and feel love and respect for these rulers. Next it elucidates exactly how a son and a daughter should act and delineates how to be a good Buddhist subject. All of this knowledge and the performance of these duties combine to make a Thai subject Thai. Each aspect of Thai-ness involves the others: Children learn their position within their family and in relation to the Royal Family, their religion, and their nation. They are instructed how to act according to the obligations inherent in these relationships. Thais are quick to describe to *farang* what "Thais" are and what "they" value.

One major contradiction in Thai-ness is that being Thai is also a racial category that excludes the majority of the residents of Thailand, although most of those ostracized consider themselves Thai and adhere to the values inherent to Thai-ness. Despite the official government explanation that Siam changed its name to Thailand because it translates as "Land of the Free," Benedict Anderson, renown political theorist for his definition of nationalism that situates most academic work in past four decades (1983), traces another reason for this name change—a way to privilege those who belonged to the Thai race. Anderson asserts that the word "Thailand" actually functions as the means for exclusion of all those who are not racially Thai but were born and live in Thailand such as the Chinese, people from Isaan (Thailand's largest and poorest area), members of Thailand's Hill Tribes, and the large Muslim population in the south.[19] Furthermore, many government policies enact racism by refusing to grant citizenship to certain hill tribes in Northern Thailand and failing to provide consistent educational standards throughout the country. This problematizes the notion of Thai-ness, because, while all residents of Thailand are taught to follow its principles and internalize its responsibilities, the system excludes many of them from full identification and accompanying benefits.

Since the beginning of Thailand's economic boom, discussions of Thai-ness in English have changed markedly; academics now evaluate conflicts and deviations within Thai identity construction. Not only are general guides about cultural practices a thriving market in English, translations of Thai literature and literary analysis are another means for the examination of themes and issues provide another means for the interpretation of Thai-ness and Thai culture in contemporary Thai literature.[20] The authors of the books describe many of the plots of these Thai short stories as centered on how modern, international life changes

19 See Anderson's "The State of Thai Studies: The Studies of the Thai State" for a description of the racism involved in the concept of Thai-ness and the contribution scholarship about Thailand has made towards developing and defining Thai-ness (1978).

20 For example, Anderson and Mendiones, *In the Mirror: Politics in Siam in the American Era* (1985), and Suvanna Kriengkraipetch and Larry E. Smith, *Value Conflicts in Thai Society: Agonies of Change Seen in Short Stories* (1992). In the latter work, analyses are grouped in the following categories: Traditions vs. Modernity, Individualism vs. Group Solidarity, New Barriers to Social Mobility, Role Conflicts of Women, and Ideological Confusion. The readings, as these headings suggest, highlight the conflicts in Thai values brought about by increased participation in the global economy.

some Thais but not others, causing clashes and misunderstandings. Although Thai nationalism is premised on the belief that "progress" is positive, Thai-ness as a defining principle that motivates all Thai people. is no longer consistent, nor positive. New actions and responses, as well as different allegiances and customs, accompany Bangkok's participation in international markets. Silkworm Press has published additional re-evaluations of Thai modernization. For example, Thongchai Winichakul's *Siam Mapped* (1994) and Pasuk Phongpaichit and Chris Baker's *Thailand* and *Thailand's Boom* (1996) and *Thai Capital after the 1997 Crisis* (2008) present historical revisions that elucidate the difficulties of incorporating western technologies while maintaining Thai culture and identity. Rosalind Morris describes "[t]he present" as "one of those times in Thailand when different and mutually irreconcilable systems cohabit in a single social field" (1994, p. 19). Thus current conditions in Thailand can reinforce, undermine, and redefine officially produced versions of what constitutes Thai-ness. For instance, an effect of globalization and the increased presence of *farang* have led to a shift in the status of *luk krung* (biracial Thais, literally "half child"). *Luk krung* used to be vociferously rejected by Thai society because they symbolized a woman's involvement with a *farang*, alluding to prostitution. Until recently, most *luk krung* born in Thailand were not considered Thai citizens and were not entitled to government mandated education or healthcare. By the 1990s, however, a large number of singers and actors in prolific music, television, and movie industries are of mixed race, and a significant number of them have been raised outside of Thailand. This marks a huge ideological shift in what is considered Thai-ness.

Each of the following chapters focuses on a specific Thai community followed by a conclusion addressing contemporary Thai stereotypes and suggesting the overall pedagogical use of these studies and the use of transnational sexuality studies in a broader contest. Below is a summary of each chapter and the community it analyzes.

Chapter Two: "Whiskey is Whiskey. You Can't Make a Cocktail from That!'": Self-Identified Gay Thai Men in Bangkok

This chapter examines the constitution of a gay identity in English by Thai men in Bangkok. Comparing accounts from interviews, newspapers, books, and magazines demonstrates that "being gay" is constructed in ways that reflect this community rather than in ways that comply with a universal model of gay identity. Economic prosperity and transnational communication have enabled self-identified gay men in Bangkok to inhabit new gendered spaces that include fresh ways of self-description and previously unavailable constructions of desire. Thus identifying as gay in Thailand can neither be reduced to western gay identity or to other forms of sexual identities and actions previously available to Thai men. It includes an awareness of the label as global, but the way in which this position is enacted in Bangkok combines and reconfigures ideologies from many sources, producing identities that are dynamic and often in conflict with each other.

Chapter Three: Tom, Dee, and *Anjaree*: "Women Who Follow Non-Conformist Ways"

During the decade of economic growth, thousands of Thai women entered the emergent middle class workforce, enjoying increased opportunities for education and the possibility of individual economic security. As a consequence, many of these women no longer deemed marriage a necessity. This chapter investigates middle class Bangkok women-who-love-women. The varied accounts by these women illustrate the instability of their positions. They employ diverse strategies for naming themselves both among each other (in Thai) and as a group within the Thai nation (in English). English-language words and phrases such as "women-who-love-women" and "lesbian" have entered Bangkok's women-who-love-women-community, yet most of its members reject these terms because they anchor identity in sex acts. Several of these women have used their knowledge of international conversations to inform their strategies for Thai community and identity formation. Anjana Suvarnananda and her organization for Thai women loving women, *Anjaree,* attempt to help women carve out identities that reflect contemporary Thai practices. Suvarnananda creates new words and communities that are in dialogue with, but not replications of, the terms and discussions of non-Thai women-who-love-women. Concurrently, Jennifer Bliss, co-editor of Bangkok's monthly *Pink Page*, describes her feelings and opinions in English to both Thai and non-Thai readers. The efforts by these women broaden this community's vocabulary and possibilities for self-description.

Chapter Four: The Weaving New Life Project: Thai Women in Official Publications

The participation of Thai women-centered Non-Government Organizations (NGOs) in transnational markets and international organizations is accompanied by the production of images of Thai women. Similarly the Thai Government disseminates romanticized images of Thai women to create a tourist friendly portrait of Thailand. These Thai women-centered organizations distribute English-language publications that target international audiences, developing processes of globalization, soliciting contributions that help rectify undesirable circumstances, and acquiring resources for educated decision-making and project implementation. Most of these organizations employ internationally recognized human rights discourses to garner support for their projects. While the images they circulate downplay sex-work, they often invoke alternative stereotypes that fall into one of two fields—aestheticized depictions of women contributing to industrial development, or romanticized portraits of women performing traditional, recognizable tasks such as weaving. While these images may extend previous assumptions about Thai women, they may also encourage greater understanding of the current conditions of women in Thailand. Rather than following these strategies, one Thai NGO encourages sex-workers to generate their own representations. Chapter Four outlines the ways in which Thai women produce texts that respond to the changing international climate, contributing to the construction of new forms of political, economic, and social participation in a global arena where women's voices were previously excluded.

Chapter Five: Import/Export: Stereotypes and Rice

This concluding section is written in a significantly different tone than the three ethnographic studies comprising Chapters Two through Four. In this chapter, I address the reader directly and survey contemporary and local sex and gender-related stereotypes of Thailand by westerners. I outline recent changes in the marketing of sex through Thai tourism. Since the twenty-first century, Thailand's tourism industry has broadened from its earlier reputation as a sex-for-sale tourist destination to quite a different haven for sex-gender related encoutners. Thailand's booming cosmetic surgery and Sex Reassigment Surgery (SRS) medical procedures are both a logical and surprising outgrowth of the sex/gender-related, Tourist of Thailand promoted, tourist market to westerners.[21] I use this example, along with a discussion of the Thai meanings of rice as cultural signifiers, to reflect on previous descriptions of sex/gender-related sub-groups provided in the preceding chapters. I then use drawings about the topics of this book done by my children to explain multiple literacies for understanding sex/sexuality/gender that inform all readers as each of us are located in specific spatio-temporal moments with a unique set of experiences that inform how we read the use of sex/gender related terms

---

21 This was told to me by a representative of the Tourism Authority of Thailand, Mr. Promate, during an interview in 2013. It is also visible on the Tourism Authority of Thailand's promoted Thailand Med Tourism: The Thailand Medical Tourist Portal: http://www.thailandmedtourism.com/Home/28.

by the groups described in the earlier chapters as well as how we interpret any new information based on how we are situated. Like the reader, each Bangkok-based group understanding, goals, and uses of language is a dialogic process always in flux and in response to the specificities of audience, location, history, and circumstances.

The importing of these English-language ideas and the resulting exports by these Thai communities expand the parameters of sex, gender, and sexualities that are often presumed fixed, legible, binary, or belonging within pre-determined categories. Each chapter examines a specific group considering their practices and Thai specific definitions of a gay identity, the effects of representations of non-western women by international organizations, the use of the terms describing women-who-love-women, and the perpetuation by the western media of stereotypes about Thai women. By documenting these translations, I provide a catalogue of current conceptions of gender, sexuality, ethnicity, nation, and globalization found in contemporary Thailand. Through these particularized studies, I hope to enlarge the reader's theoretical understandings of international market participation and the articulations of genders and sexualities. Ultimately, I ask that readers consider this study as the production of knowledges, not truths about what Thai people think or are. Chapter Five challenges readers to use the contents of this book as a way to encounter Thailand but also, more importantly, to take this discussion about the use of English-language terms for sex and gender by specific groups of Thais in Bangkok as a challenge to sustain this consideration. Moving beyond the boundaries of Thailand, I suggest a continued query of the strategies, stereotypes, and multiple interpretations of any sex/gender related construct posited as fixed, pre-determined, and/or natural.

By updating and framing the ethnographic studies I conducted in the between 1993 and 2004, *Import Export: English Language Genders in Thailand* provides a contribution to the growing body of work concerning gender and sexuality in Southeast Asia. By focusing on these small Bangkok-based communities, I offer extended research to a small canon of studies focuses specifically on Thailand. This book offers theoretical models that may serve as the basis of comparisons with other groups in the region. Moreover, by contextualizing this work within the framework of the increasingly popular topic of transnational sexuality studies, I hope to suggest new questions, procedures, and ways of thinking when considering, more broadly, the vicissitudes of language, representation, and transnational imports and exports.

2

"Whiskey is Whiskey. You Can't Make a Cocktail from That!": Self-Identified Gay Thai Men in Bangkok

"Men who are not a part of Bangkok's gay culture see things only as they are," announced Law (not his real name), a self-identified gay Thai man who frequents Bangkok's gay clubs and bars and manages a Thai restaurant that caters to gay *farang* (western) clientele. Law teaches his staff what westerners expect in a meal, providing traditional Thai food tempered to *farang* tastes and presented in the European manner with appetizer, soup, entree, and dessert, and an extensive wine list from which he offers recommendations that complement each order. Law understands *farang* culture, he declared, because becoming gay has made him creative and able to comprehend and change things around him. According to Law, a Thai man who is not gay sees whiskey and wants to drink it just as it is, never considering alternative drinks that make life better, more beautiful, and more interesting. Law is one of many Thai men in Bangkok who speaks English as much as possible, dates only *farang* men, and considers himself gay. However, the way he describes being gay neither coincides with the identifications of his boyfriends nor his other self-identified gay Thai friends.

In the past ten years, many representations of gayness have been produced in Bangkok. This chapter examines some of these representations, showing how different sources in Bangkok constitute being gay to the English-speaking community. Rather than imagining the existence of a "universal" model of gay identity that men around the world adopt or invoking the universal grammar sometimes applied to incongruous sites by post-colonial theory, this essay documents some of the alternative models of gayness described by Thai men, illustrating how the "ingredients" of the "cocktail" Law suggested are not prefigured or consistent, even within this small, recently constructed community.[22]

22 Dennis Altman critiques Michael Warner's position in *Fear of a Queer Planet*: "American 'queer theory' remains as relentlessly Atlantic-centric in its view of the world as the mainstream culture it critiques." (418). He then posits that "if we abandon the idea that the model for the rest of the world--whether political, cultural, or intellectual--need be New York or Paris, and if we recognize the emerging possibilities for such models in Bangkok and Harare, we may indeed be able to speak of 'a queer planet'" ("Global" 1997, p. 433). Altman (1997 and 2001), Lawrence Cohen (1998), and Martin F. Manalansan IV (1994) all launch the same sort of critiques of queer theory: "In a world where borders are coming undone and 'gay' ideologies, practices, and images are tracing the trajectories of modernity, the globalization of the gay movement has proven to be problematic" (1994, p. 425). "Both mass media and popular opinion have long taken for granted that gay and lesbian culture and politics have spread worldwide" (Manalansan, 1994 p. 425).

Self-identified gay Thai men participating in Bangkok's gay community create and inhabit new gendered spaces that reflect Thailand's ten-year economic boom and its increasing participation in international markets. In the process, they provide new self-descriptions and presentations. Western gay identities do not prefigure being gay in Thailand, nor does the position of *kathoey* (Thai transsexuals and transvestites) or the terms Thai men-who-have-sex-with-men use to describe their actions. Positioning oneself as gay in Thailand includes an awareness of the label as global, but the ways in which it is enacted combines and repositions ideologies from many sources, producing many diverse, dynamic, often conflicting descriptions, as well as altering and increasing erotic possibilities and avenues for articulating desire.

As a result of Thailand's economic boom, the number and types of venues for entertainment have swelled.[23] Most of these venues target particular clienteles, and my study focuses on those frequented by customers who consider themselves gay. The self-identified gay men that I refer to spend at least several nights a week at Bangkok's most popular gay nightclub, DJ Station, located on one of the two alleys known for gay clubs and restaurants. The gay community that these men describe includes specific bars, gyms, restaurants, and clubs. Many of these sites are located between Suriwong and Silom Roads, just above the notorious "brothel" district, Patpong, where *farang* go to pick up women and shop at the night bazaar. Below Patpong is an alley containing many "off-bars" where *farang* and other non-Thais purchase the services of men.

---

23 See Chapter One for a full account of Thailand's ten-year economic boom.

DJ Station, and many of the other bars and saunas, have been created recently and their numbers keep increasing, spreading to other areas of Bangkok. The clubs follow many of the patterns of western gay bars, with high priced mixed drinks and beer, technologically advanced dance floors, interiors carefully constructed with attention to detail and DJs, but they are also specifically Thai. The floorshow seems both universal and specific, in moments, to the Thai audience. Each night dance performances by muscle-bodied gay men and highly stylized feminine chanteuses, *kathoey,* are interspersed with Thai or regional language skits that originate from classic tales normally performed in local village fairs. Thus *farang* see what they expect while sections of the show are specifically speaking to Thai audiences And the system of buying a bottle and keeping it at the bar so one can be admitted without cover charge is international, but also specifically an urban Thai practice prevalent in Bangkok as a way of inviting return clientele and becoming "VIP" (an important status designation to Thais). The majority of the Thai men who participate in this community and go to these places work in the western oriented service industry. While this industry continues to expand, it does not employ a large percentage of the Thai work force in Bangkok.[24] My most extensive interviews, and the bulk of the quotes discussed in this essay, come from several men with whom I spent a great deal of time over a ten-month period (August 1995- May1996). My archive includes informal discussions with over forty self-identified

---

24 By the western oriented service industry, I mean hotels, restaurants, and other local spaces designed to serve western clientele located in Bangkok. Banks, international corporations, educational institutions, the Transportation Authority and construction agencies are a few of the industries in Bangkok that employ a greater percentage of the Thai work force.

gay Thai men and twelve formal interviews, as well as discussions with approximately fifteen western men involved in this scene. I have also traced the representation of gayness in Thailand in English-language texts available in Bangkok during the period of my research.

These men are central in my analysis. Law, originally from Isaan, the poorest region in northeast Thailand, managed the restaurant described above. Jin, also from Isaan, worked as a cook at a famous international hotel before he started working in an exclusive men's club for fitness and relaxation with an international clientele. Oat, a young Bangkok native, attends a local university studying German and tourism. Joe is a westerner who works for a Bangkok advertising firm and has lived in Bangkok for four years. He and Oat had a relationship that lasted over a year, and at the time of these interviews they, and the other men, were close friends.

Although most of the men who are a part of this community refer to themselves as gay, there are many other terms that describe men having sex with men in Thai. Dutch Professor Jan W. de Lind van Wijngaarden, an expert on HIV infection and prevention in Asian countries, reports 29 different Thai words for male homoerotic desire and actions from interviews with only 51 informants. Despite this large number of terms, each possesses a unique signification. Rather than constituting identities, most of these terms focus on the actions of these men. According to the men I interviewed, the performance of these acts does not necessarily change how they envision their sexual identity. Similarly, the contributors to *The Men of Thailand Guide to Thailand* have asserted, "Although male-to-male sexual behavior is universal, an identity based on it is not. It has only been within the past five years that a clearer distinction about what it means to be gay (as opposed to being *kathoey*—effeminate, transvestite, trans-sexual) has formed" (Allyn, 1995, p. 57). Imagining the advent of this international gay community in either/or fashion, as an acceptance and co-option of a seamless western gay identity or as a Thai indigenization that provides more words for actions without the incorporation of identity construction, simplifies what takes place. Instead, various western images, ideologies, bodies, and languages are influencing the ways in which self-identified gay Thai men construct and describe being gay. The articulation of this modern construction is not consistent among its members, illustrating that even within this single, isolated community, the ways in which new positions are described and adopted are uneven and multifarious.

English is the most common language for communication by self-identified gay Thai men with *farang*. The quote I provided by Allyn and Jackson in my previous chapter helps explain its usage. "English has an exotic and cultured sense for many Thais, having associations with wealth, education, culture, modernity, and sexual liberality" (1995, p. 236). Not only have the *Bangkok Post* and the *Nation*, Thailand's two largest daily English-language newspapers, begun to print many international wire service stories about sexuality, gender, and gays outside of Thailand, but also sexuality and sexual practices in Thailand, by both *farang* in Thailand and Thais, are increasingly being described and interpreted.

Peter Jackson, described as "an Australian researcher…whose work has shed light on the phenomenon of the Thai cross-dresser," presenting his history and explanation of the position of *kathoey* in Thai society (Kanjanawanawan, 1995, p. 31), has stated, "Thailand is a society where having sex is relatively unsanctioned, but talking about it in public is strongly sanctioned," (1999, p. 14) this public silence has diminished partially as a result of the increasing prevalence of *farang* and *farang* products in addition to English-language presses. Because non-Thai speakers are involved in greater numbers of economic, including sexual, interactions in Bangkok, English has become a dominant language used by Thais with both other Thais and non-Thais. Because the widespread use of English is recent—a product of Thailand's entrance into international markets—targeting English-language representations reveals the effects of globalization. The representations are central to understanding what constitutes being a self-identified gay Thai man.

An increased curiosity and openness to foreign ideas accompanies the desire for imported products in Bangkok, evident in the changing styles of clothing, movies, and popular music. Both imported and Thai-produced goods and services reflect interests in trends and practices that previously occurred or were discussed outside of Thailand's borders.[25] For example, Suwatana Aribarg, a psychiatrist and professor of Chulalongkorn's Medical School Faculty, the most esteemed medical school in Thailand, explained in a 1995 interview that Thai society was previously silent about non-heterosexual practices, "Homosexuality

---

25 One interesting result is the popularity of *luk krung* (biracial Thais, literally "half child"). See Chapter One for further details.

is inherent in every culture, every society. It's not a result of Western influence as some say. Homosexuality may be less of an open presence in Thai society…because Thais regard sexuality as an embarrassing matter that shouldn't be openly discussed or flaunted" (1995, p. 31). However, as a result of the widespread presence of *farang* products and ideas, sex, and sexualities in *farang* senses have become subjects sanctified for scrutiny and discussion. *The Men of Thailand's Guide to Thailand* reports this economic boom and its resulting change in the way men meet men:

In mid 1994, the trend became clear. A Thai gay identity is being born in a non-homophobic society. A sign of this was reflected in its gay businesses. … There was also an astonishing surge in the number of gay venues without male sex workers. … Some may think that the Thai gay world is developing, but we think it is evolving to meet the needs of Thai gay men.[26]

This passage clearly yokes the "surge in the number of gay venues" to "the needs of Thai gay men." Although the men I interviewed unanimously contradicted the assertion that Thailand is "non-

---

26 *The Men Of Thailand Guide To Thailand* p. 6. Despite the claims made by this assertion, and although Thailand is remarkably less homophobic than many countries (illustrated by the common acknowledgement that three of the Thai Prime Ministers in the last twenty years have been known to have sex with men), self-identified gay Thai men still face homophobia and discrimination for several reasons: initially AIDS was presented as a "gay disease," and Thai men with *farang* are often assumed to be sex-workers worthy of disdain. Because of the relative silence about sexual actions, many *farang* believe that Thailand is a non-homophobic society, thus Thailand is often depicted by non-Thais as a gay paradise and many tourists come to Thailand specifically for this reason. By perceiving silence as freedom, visitors often do not realize the potential isolation, condemnation, and rejection Thais can face when they do not fulfill their parents' expectations as a result, either directly or indirectly, of their participation in the gay community.

homophobic," the emergence of gay businesses and venues, as well as the change in the types of services offered, links economic success in an international market to the desires of Thai gay men. *The Men of Thailand Guide* jubilantly pronounced 1986 the year *farang* labeled Thailand a "gay paradise," but it also claimed that the scene was "evolving," not "developing," and that it evolved according to Thai needs rather than *farang* desires. The refusal to attribute this to "development" recognizes that such a term would insinuate an uncritical replication of western structures. Proposing evolution based on the needs of Thai gay men presents an example of what Arjun Appadurai described as "a space of contestation in which individuals and groups seek to annex the global into their own practices of the modern" (1997, p. 4). Oat similarly remarked on Bangkok society's increasing awareness and acceptance of the appearance of western style gay culture, "Ten years ago, straight people didn't accept [the presence of gays] as much as now, but now they are open-minded and accept it. We live in the capital city" (Oat, personal communication, 1995). His positioning of Bangkok as central and capital within Thailand acknowledges it as the location where new ideas and experiences emerge.

Coinciding with the arrival of new ideas and practices is the expansion in the number and types of players in Thailand's economic growth and urbanization, increasing the opportunities for economically disadvantaged and less-educated families to achieve economic prosperity. Thai men from poor families often make their way to Bangkok to find work. If they master basic English and learn some *farang* habits and expectations, they may be able to obtain a job in one of many businesses catering to *farang* clientele that pays a salary large enough to enable family support. Participation in the gay community by having relationships with *farang* also provides economic opportunities: Thai men can learn English and understand *farang* cultures, make business contacts and find lucrative employment, and possibly secure direct economic support for themselves and their families. Dennis Altman has written of Asian men in Thailand and Indonesia:

> Without denying the ugliness born of larger economic inequities, one has to recognize a somewhat more complex pattern of relationships at work. In many cases young men are able to use their sexual contacts with (usually older) foreigners to win entry into the western world, either through the acquisition of money, skills, or language or, more dramatically, the possibility of emigration. (Altman, 1997, p. 428)

As Altman has argued, the frequent inequities of both money and power in Asian/western relationships have complex results, often providing young men with economic and educational opportunities.

Law excluded himself from the following generalization and then stated, "Thai gay men are concerned with money, economy. They mostly come from poor families. Being gay is easy money, so they don't care about relationships except for money" (Law, personal communication, 1996). In the same manner, Oat excluded himself when asked about the economic motivation for Thai men to have relationships with *farang*.

He said, "For myself...I don't care about someone being white, black, etcetera, as long as he is good." When his relationship with his partner, Joe, ended, his self-identified gay Thai friends, including Law, said he "should find another westerner, a rich one so they can pay me. They advised me to have a relationship for that reason only, but I didn't follow their advice." He thinks the only motivation of some Thai men to be gay is financial. He explained, "Some of them don't work, just wait for westerners. Some of them who look really nice and just go to the bars and look for westerners" [sic]. And like Law, Oat codes economic dependence as pejorative. "I don't mean that all Thai gay men are all bad, just some. Thai gay men who deal with westerners need money from westerners. They can sponsor their life..." (Oat, personal communication, 1996). This separation of the speaker from the subject matter—the manner in which Law and Oat describe material gain as a motivation for the men around them but not for themselves—illustrates that assumptions and generalizations could affect what they "really see." Before the boom, Thai relationships with *farang* often took the form of sex-worker/customer, and this history could affect their interpretations. That neither one of them perceives their relationships with *farang* as an example of this dynamic suggests several things. First, not all interracial relationships are primarily based on unidirectional economic gain. Second, Oat and Law deploy a non-economic normative notion that relationships should be romantic and sexual only. This deviates from standard Thai ideology that deems economics one central factor of a relationship.

Law believes that his relationship with Hans enables him to

obtain knowledge about the west, which also increases his chances for financial success in the increasingly global Thai economy. Hans concurs, explaining that he plans to take Law with him back to Denmark in the future. Hans, a Danish businessman in his early forties, has been visiting Thailand for increasing lengths of time over the past several years. The couple have considered themselves to be in a relationship since the night they first met at DJ Station Although they celebrate their meeting as their anniversary, Hans was, in fact, at the bar with another Thai "boyfriend" that night, and it was eight months after this night when Hans asked Law to be in an exclusive relationship. Law states that he wants to learn and change while in this relationship, so he frequently solicits advice from Hans and tries to understand his values and aesthetics. He accepts Hans' anniversary date, despite his other Thai tie that night, as he adapts to become fluent in Hans' culture and practices.

Law believes this relationship has changed his personality; for example, he no longer covets possessions. He explained, "Before I was gay, I was…jealous about people having more than me and competitive. Now I'm more easygoing and jealous about relationships, but not what others have" (Law, personal communication, 1995). During the course of this long distance, long-term relationship (over two years), he has never taken money directly from Hans. And some of the economic interactions that accompany the relationship are reciprocal. Recently, they collaborated on a business transaction in which Hans provided an artist's brass candelabra that Law arranged to mass-produce in a Thai factory. Subsequently the mass-produced objects were sold in Denmark. Hans also invested the capital for their production and consequently received the majority of the profit. This cooperative collaboration illustrates the dynamic and diverse interactions of market and interpersonal relations within the Thai/*farang* gay community of Bangkok.

Although there is a pattern, some Thai/*farang* relationships alter the economic dynamics. For example, Jin and Joe had a brief relationship concurrent to Jin's other long-term commitment. While the latter replicated the stereotypical dynamic—Jin received economic support and increased possibilities for prestigious employment such as a job cooking in the premiere international hotel in Bangkok—the former served as a kind of reversal. When with Joe, Jin insisted on paying for all the meals they shared. He also frequently bought Joe clothes and gifts; one time he filled Joe's room with flowers. This positioned him as the "older brother" who has more money and more prestige than the younger. While sibling relationships that privilege age and social position exist between all Thais, *farang* frequently receive superior status despite their frequent ignorance of the existence of this type of social relationship and the obligations it entails. By adopting the role of older brother, Jin reframed the social and economic hierarchy usually found in Thai/*farang* relationships, mixing mainstream Thai conventions and the gay community's practices, creating a variation in both.

Negotiating Identities

Thailand's participation in global marketplaces definitely contributes to the establishment of an international gay scene that manifests itself in a manner that reflects Bangkok's history and the changing opportunities for economic advancement. Like the concept of a gay identity, the current construction of Thai identity—although more explicitly delineated—is also a conflicted position. Self-identified gay Thai men inhabit both positions—being Thai and being gay—despite some procedures that are in opposition, such as the privileging of youth in the gay community and the increased status afforded to age in most Thai communities. Those who embody this position are currently exploring through literature and popular press how one can be both Thai and gay, or a gay Thai.

The simplicity and conformity of explanations of Thai identity belie the often-conflicted obligations it requires. Thai attachment to family, society, royalty, and religion is repeatedly premised as the most crucial aspect of Thai-ness.[27] Imbued with the responsibilities inherent in Thai-ness, Law is very concerned about his position in his family; he says that first and foremost he wants to be a good Thai son and feels guilty that he ignored his parents' request to marry.[28] Consequently, he puts most of his salary toward the construction of an exquisite house for his parents. It includes fixtures imported from Europe and a greenhouse for orchids. This is exorbitant in his small, tropical village consisting of

---

27 See Chapter One for a more extensive consideration of Thai-ness.

28 Law and two other men from his village, as well as other Thai men in this community, find it important to build homes for their parents. This was formerly an obligation reserved for daughters. This illustrates that the expectations for being a good Thai are also changing because, at least in part, of the increased opportunities for economic advancement. Historically, daughters and their husbands would inhabit and eventually inherit the parents' home and land. Thus it was their duty, and in their best interest, to improve it. Now, the child who achieves the most economic success should improve the lives of his/her parents.

two dirt roads, a temple, rice fields, and other rudimentary homes that possess neither running water nor plumbing. By doing this, he fulfills the primary Thai obligation of showing respect to his parents, exceeding their expectations and incorporating his own.

While this feeling of commitment and interconnectedness begins at the level of family, it extends past the family and incorporates religion and nationalism. Being Thai is a developed, explained, and promoted identity in Thailand. Intertwined with Thai-ness is Thai nationalism. The two qualities seem almost identical, but Thai nationalism, *Chat Thai*, was an addition during the reign of King Vijiravudh (23 October 1910 – 26 November 1925). Esteemed Thai historian David K. Wyatt has written, "He saw the nation as a corporate body of people, imbued with a common identity, striving for common purposes, placing the commonweal[th] ahead of private interests" (1984, p. 229). Historian Scot Barme has further demonstrated that the royal ruling elite's construction of Thai nationalism, taught to schoolchildren since the beginning of the twentieth century, bound it to progress and civilization—two positively perceived concepts that were promoted during the reign of the previous king. [29] Wyatt has asserted "a single theme that runs through the whole reign" is "King Vijiravudh's idea of the 'Thai nation'"(1984, p. 229).

In his famous 1954 Thai-language novel, *Four Reigns*, Kukrit Pramoj has one of the king's elite subjects, Khun Prem, describe how the King has inspired a nationalistic feeling:

---

29 See Scot Barme's essay, "Luang Wichit Wathakan and the Creation of a Thai Identity" for a full explanation of the linking of Thai nationalism, progress, and civilization.

> Sometimes I have this feeling...that all the love I
> have for my wife, my children, my clan, my country,
> all this is there in my love for him and that I can do
> everything for him including giving up my life. It's this
> love that spurs me on, my personal ambition is mixed
> up in it and so is my wish to improve myself so that I
> could be of greater service to the nation, be a worthy
> servant of him who leads all of us in serving the nation.
> (1999, p. 149)[30]

Thai nationalism is thereby constructed as something that is imposed upon the people by their leaders that requires direct identification with and devotion to the nation and its rulers rather than recognition of one's interconnectedness and the obligations this entails. Consequently, feelings of nationalism are sometimes so intense that their expression takes on, from a western gaze, erotic tones. Khun Prem expressed his love for King Vajiravudh thus "When he's in a gay mood, playful, mischievous, laughing, and teasing and joking with friends, smiling his beautiful smile, then I'm completely enthralled, utterly under his spell. You might have said I'd fallen madly in love with him as though he were a girl. When he's in this mood to be with him is pure enchantment" (Pramoj, 1999, p. 150). Kukrit presents many levels for the love of Khun Prem for his king,

---

30 This novel, originally serialized in a Thai newspaper and later appearing in book form in both Thai and English as well as in TV serial form, is the most well known in Thailand. Written by a famous statesman and covering four reigns of kings as well as the brief period without a monarchy, it traces the life of the virtuous Thai woman, Ploi, and her family. While it was printed as a novel in Thai in 1954, its English translation, by Tulachandra, had no publishing date until it was reprinted, pagination the same as original edition, by Silkworm Press in 1999.

but at this moment his emotions for the king are youthful and erotic. He feels "sorrow," "pity," "enthralled," "under his spell" and "madly in love." This remarkable passage moves from a deep sense of devotion, passionately articulating his feelings of nationalism towards the king to a testament of infatuation. It is carefully described, but then moved past. The narrator, Khun Prem's wife, makes no comment about the effusive emotions that constitute her husband's feeling of nationalism. Intense sentiment and love for one's king is an aspect of manliness. As Law has explained, Thai society expects men to express strong emotions.

Many of the men I interviewed may not feel a lot of tension from their existence in these two seemingly incommensurate communities because of the physical distance that exists between them. Most of the men who participate in the Bangkok gay scene have emigrated from rural areas to Bangkok, and one requirement of Thai-ness is to recognize the place where your family comes from as your home. Thus, while living in Bangkok they are not located in their native Thai community. When returning to their homes and families, they leave behind the gay community in Bangkok. In contrast, Oat returns to his suburban Bangkok home and family almost nightly. His two communities overlap in his daily life, moving from home and university to work in Law's restaurant or going out to DJ Station. Law is an exception to the other self-identified gay Thai men I interviewed because he incorporates his gay life with his time at home. Hans has visited Law's family several times, as did a previous *farang* boyfriend, and, though they always share a mat and mosquito net when sleeping in the public space (this is not necessarily unusual among Thai friends), Law has received no direct comments or condemnation from his family. His parents, brothers, sister, and extended family welcome visits from Law's friends. Hence, while Law's communities do not interact on a daily basis like Oat's, he still manages to combine them and claims that the only conflict lies in his refusal to honor the request, only spoken once by his mother and father, to marry.

This coexistence of clashing systems is reflected in Oat's ambivalence towards his participation in what he sees as two irreconcilable communities. He envisions a future that follows the expectations of mainstream Thai society, coding it as inevitable rather than as a choice. "I think it's a kind of social fact that one day you have to get married and have a child. I think it's kind of like being human" (Oat, personal communication, 1995). While many Thai men who have sex with men but do not identify themselves as gay are able to fulfill these obligations, I met no married self-identified gay men. As an answer to my repeated queries as to why he continually opposed men to gays and explained them as different from one another (1996). He stated: "I think a man is a man and a gay is a kind of man who has sex with a man and who can love a man" (Oat, personal communication, 1996). Thus while men may describe strong emotions, gay men occupy a different category than men. All men should have strong emotions; gay men are a specific "kind of man."

Oat felt pressure to leave the gay community rather than fuse his participation and identity as a Thai gay man so that he can fulfill what he considers to be the obligations of being Thai. "Since I am now older than twenty, I have to make plans for my life." (Oat, personal communication, 1996). However, he still enjoys participating in the gay community from which he has gained much; his excellent skills in English and increased self-confidence have enabled him to qualify as an official, licensed tour guide, win the prestigious and competitive title, Young Leader of Thailand,[31] and land a high salaried job. However, he privileges his Thai-ness over his participation in the gay community in his plans for his future.

Law, on the other hand, says that he does not feel that his two identities or his participation in two communities produce conflict or contradiction. In fact, he believes being gay has made him better able to perform his duties as a Thai. He illustrated his success by recounting how he kept his younger relatives occupied and how he convinced them that washing could be fun. "One day when the kids were in the way while the adults were working, I set up a basketball game complete with a goal by using two chairs. When they don't want to take a shower, I make the hose like a rainstorm that they can play in—then they all take showers." (Law, personal communication, 1995). Rather then scolding the children or forcing them to wash despite their displeasure, Law finds new solutions that engage and entertain them. This creative thinking he attributes to being gay. Similarly, the house that Law designed for his parents does

---

31 This included the opportunity for international travel and both national and international recognition. Oat's achievement was announced in the Thai and English-language presses, as well as presses in Singapore, and he received an all expense paid trip to Singapore to meet with other Young Leaders and government officials from many Asian nations.

not conform to the current custom of demolishing old teak houses to install new, modern houses of cement. Instead he has refurbished the teak from the original house and built a much larger house with little cement and the outward appearance of a traditional Thai teak house. The European innovations he includes are consistent with his own aesthetics and in dialogue with the increasing interest shown by some Thais for historical preservation, yet opposed to mainstream procedures for home renovation.[32] These examples show the importance Law places on his commitment to his family, but rather than following expected procedures, he fulfills his commitments in non-conventional ways. Law repeatedly attributes his appreciation of Thai history and architectural traditions, as well as his impulses to devise creative solutions, to his membership in the gay community as well as the tutelage provided by Hans.

Law also notes that there are situations in which being gay and the practices that it entails are in opposition with Thai tradition. He recounts that most of his friends increasingly rely on financial support from their boyfriends:

> Gai is really country and still spends a lot of time there. He doesn't need much. Steven gives money, instead of "helping" him. It makes Gai dependent directly on Steven.

---

32 Thais increasingly consider their ruins and traditional wooden structures to be important aesthetic achievements, enjoyable to visit and worth preserving rather than neglecting or destroying for modern constructions. This is promoted by the Tourism Authority of Thailand, which started to designate ruins as national monuments, promoting them as important historical sites and investing in their upkeep to increase tourism. While sometimes considered a strategy pandering to western tourists' expectations and practices (Thai people historically visited temples with famous monks), many Thai people are starting to visit ruins, and repair, rather than renovate, Thai temples.

In Jep's case, John will give Jep money to study or whatever he wants to do. But Jep is starting to take advantage of it. Recently, he enrolled in three English classes and never went. And Jin is going to lose Shawn because he cheats on him all the time, even though he needs his support. (Law, personal communication, 1996)

Law recognizes that the Bangkok gay community privileges youth and worries that his friends may not realize this because the Thai society endows status on increasing age. These contradictory positions of respect mark an instance where being gay and being Thai do not mesh. Law finds that his friends perceive their current positions within the two as stable, while he believes that decisions they make now will affect how they will be perceived and what opportunities will be available to them in a future where social roles are continually shifting and changing.

Only Law has described "being gay" as a particular sex act with a *farang* man. He identifies his initial sexual encounter with Hans, although not his first time having sex with a man, as the moment when he "became gay." He stated:

I think my first serious relationship was with a *farang* man. My first real gay sex was with a westerner, but before that I fooled around with Thai guys. Sometimes we liked each other and we hung around together. With some men I liked we would do a kind of touching, but it was never like really making love. So the first time I should say, was with a westerner. And it just happened. I didn't say I wanted to have a relationship with a westerner. I

cannot say why I did it, because at that time everything
was going perfect for me. So when the opportunity came,
I didn't deny it and I didn't panic. I just let it happen.
(Law, personal communication, 1999)

Following this, he provided the details of his arrival at the hotel, the seduction, the sex act, and the aftermath. In this account, he did not describe previous sexual encounters with other men as "really making love," yet he did have sex with them. In accordance with other Thai descriptions, Law does not code sexual interactions with Thai men as gay. But Law related a sex act as the reason for his gay identification or as an experience that led to his participation in the gay community. The length of his involvement with Hans and his yearly visits to Denmark may account for his response to this question, as well as many of his self-descriptions in which he aligns himself more closely with *farang* gay culture than his friends do.

None of the other men narrated a particular sex act or marked sexual desire as the determining factor of being gay. Most attributed their identification to community involvement, as opposed to sexual identification or desire. This involvement may be premised on a variety of conditions: some men cited their work in a western-oriented service industry, others their habit of recreating at Bangkok's gay saunas or clubs such as DJ Station, several associated being gay with their interest in travelling, befriending *farang* men, or some other type of participation in an aspect of western culture. Most, but not all, revealed that they had previous sexual encounters with men, some Thai and some non-Thai.

Their answers did not conform to either the habitual Thai practice of employing an illustrative term to describe a specific sexual action rather than assuming a sexual identity nor to the western gay tendency to "come out." Instead of sexual desire or a defining sex act, the majority linked being gay to participation in some form of gay community. Both Law and Oat remark separately that what makes them identify as gay "is intensely personal" and is not mirrored by other Thai men in the community. This may be partially attributed to their position as informants, but they also stand apart from the gay community because of their long-term relationships, relatively secure and well-paid employment, and intensive knowledge of English and *farang* cultures.

None of the men I talked to mentioned penetration as a factor in determining their gay identity. This is surprising in light of other research that finds penetration the distinguishing factor for marking gay male identity. For instance, anthropologist Lawrence Cohen wrote of his informant, "Chicano male homosociality for Tomas Amaguer is encompassed by the two bordering systemizations—gay/straight and *activo/pasivo*—that his informants negotiate" (1998, p. 424). And the transvestite, third-gendered *travesti* in Brazil interviewed by Don Kulick in his book, *Travesti* (1998), the first sustained academic manuscript dedicated to a single transgender population, consistently described being penetrated, most often by a "heterosexual" man, as the assumed position when having sex.[33] Similarly, sexual encounters involving

---

33 This is described in many interviews that appear in his book. For Kulick's interpretation, see pages 47-60 (1998). For more discussions about active/passive positions and penetration, see *Third Sex Third Gender*, edited by Gilbert Herdt (1994).

kathoey, Thailand's third-gendered transsexuals and transvestites, assume an active/passive encounter, and the men who penetrate *kathoey* are understood to be performing a heterosexual act. Since none of the men that I interviewed mentioned their position as a determinant for considering themselves gay, I must assume that, at least for these men, penetration is not a significant factor. This variation illustrates that being gay in Bangkok is a historically specific position reflecting an amalgamation of conceptions and practices.

The respondents' difficulty in comprehending my query after a general definition of "being gay" and their requests for further elucidation suggest that delineating their position was not a necessary procedure to inhabiting it. Law excluded his friends when explaining what being gay means to him. "When I speak about gayness I talk only about myself, not them. Maybe what I have been through is different because I met very different people" (Law, personal communication, 1995). During the course of the interviews, the way he constructed being gay varied tremendously; frequently he defined it as social, describing being gay through encounters, experiences, and things he learned from western gay men. He asserted that being gay provides him with new abilities, but he would also, at times, credit his "improvements" as deriving from the knowledge provided by Hans. Similarly, Oat attributed his increased self-confidence to being gay, while at other times he declared it was a result of his long-term relationship with his *farang* boyfriend and, later, close friend, Joe. Despite their reference to community involvement, other men I interviewed analogously attributed what they sensed as personal growth to the *farang* with whom they first assumed a gay identification.

Although he described himself as changed because of his involvement in the gay community and his relationship with Joe, Oat sometimes refused the moniker "gay," resisting the western term and the attempts by *farang* to classify him. He suggested that it is a *farang* obsession and complained that *farang* he knew had prescribed the position for him, despite his refusal:

> I talked about this to many westerners. Somebody said, okay you are gay. But I don't feel gay. But I feel bisexual. Somebody said I am gay even if I feel bisexual because I never have/had [tense unclear] sex with women, so how can I be bisexual if I've never have sex with women. But I am Thai, and I still believe that kind of Thai attitude that you can't have sex with a Thai woman until you marry her. I don't go to prostitutes because I don't want to, though someone said if I don't go and I get married, I won't know how to make love. But I already know how to make love. So I don't have sex with women, but I call myself bisexual anyway. (Oat, personal communication, 1996)

By describing himself as bisexual despite his lack of experience with women, he revealed both his anxiety that being gay is incompatible with his future plans and his membership within traditional Thai society, as well as his resistance to western categorizations. Oat dismissed *farang* attempts to assign him an identity based on his sexual history. Despite pressure from his friends to have sex with a sex-worker, he declared that he "already know[s] how to make love," insinuating that sex with *farang* men will prepare him for sex with Thai women. He did not accept the label "gay" despite his actions—he consistently had sex and relationships with *farang* men, he was an active member of the gay community, frequenting gay bars, clubs, and restaurants, and he worked in the *farang*-oriented service sector—the qualifications presented by other Thai men to describe being gay. This marked his resistance to *farang* pressure, his refusal to accept an identity based on his current actions, and his concern that being gay would affect his ability to be Thai. Oat's fluctuation in his self-description illustrates one strategy for managing what he perceived as a contested, inconsistent, and contradictory position. Other strategies exist, and the possibilities are proliferating.

"It's Time for The Show!"[34]

Instances where self-identified gay Thai men's presentations address practices of *farang* gays, resisting, adapting, and accepting elements of what they perceive as "international gay culture" frequently occured at locations considered part of the gay community. While *kathoey*, Thai "lady-boys" who were born with male bodies but believe they possess women's souls and cross-dress or surgically feminize their bodies, have accepted positions in rural, lower-class Thai society (Thai studies scholar Rosalind Morris problematically describes *kathoey* as

---

34 Since the time of my research, the Thai economy has taken a drastic turn for the worse. The Baht, Thailand's monetary unit, was allowed to float freely and has dropped drastically in value on the international exchange. As a result, the I.M.F. began a bailout in December 1997.

inhabiting a "biologically irreducible third category"[35]), self-identified gay men created identities and positions vis-á-vis middle-class Thai society. Despite their different histories and representations, *kathoey* and self-identified gay Thai men currently coexist in the Bangkok gay community and in English-language representations. Moreover, English-language accounts of *kathoey* have increased markedly since the emergence of a Thai gay community. Comparing new notions of what constitutes being gay with the more established, yet dynamic, positions held by *kathoey* reveals additional elements that affect Thai conceptions of gayness as well as providing strategies for the imagining of a gay Thai identity as coexisting and compatible with Bangkok upper-class norms.

DJ Station, the most popular gay club in Bangkok, was packed in the mid- to late- 90s every night with Thais and *farang* eager to interact. Yet that was not the only purpose of the evening for the Thai men in attendance. Each night at about eleven, a special song blasted through the speakers announcing the beginning of "The Show."[36] Almost all the Thai men present gathered around the stage and chant, in English, "It's time for the show!" When the music stopped and the lights dimmed, they cheered in anticipation. Most evenings, the show began with a male

---

35 "Three Sexes," 1994, p. 19. See this essay for a description of the history and position of *kathoey* in Thai society. For a discussion in which she complicates this strong assertion, revising her assertion that *kathoey* constitute a third sex, as well as providing additional analysis, refer to her more recent essay, "Educating Desire" (1997). More general descriptions of *kathoey* and how they are positioned in mainstream Thai society can be found in Peter Jackson's *Dear Uncle Go* (1995) and Allyn's *The Men of Thailand Guide to Thailand* (1995).

36 Describing the current state of Thailand's economy, Teera Phutrakul, director of a Thai mutual fund, told the *New York Times*, "Once you call the I.M.F., the party's over" (Friedman, 1997). The following description of "The Show" occurred when "the party" was in full swing.

Master of Ceremonies (MC), dressed haphazardly in women's clothes, addressing the audience in Thai. If s/he spoke English at all, it was normally as a joke. After the introduction, *kathoey*, and self-identified gay Thai men performed choreographed dances to four or five songs—some hits from Europe and the United States, some from Thailand's prolific music industry. Each show also featured a spoof of a traditional Thai tale.

One performance was inspired by a romance about a maiden who fell in love with a poor buffalo tender. Because her parents hoped the maiden would find a husband who had a higher position in society, thereby raising the family's status and wealth, they forbade their daughter to follow her heart . As in most iterations of this tale, the lovers continued to meet and the relationship blossomed. "It's very romantic," Law emphasized when describing the traditional plot. In the version performed at DJ Station, the maiden was played by an older, skinny man who, dressed in the traditional Thai women's garb, appeared ugly and crass. The buffalo was played by a heavy man wearing only ragged diaper-like shorts, crawling on his hands and knees, and making sounds and movements more like a pig than a man or a buffalo. Another actor was riding him and playing the flute. The enactment proceeded as follows: The old, ugly, disheveled "woman" pretended to take off her clothes and wrap herself in a sarong. She exposed fake pubic hair (colored fuzzy material) and breasts that were saggy, sack-like balloons wrapped in panty hose and pinned on a bra. She blew up a condom and acted as if she was releasing the air into her vagina. Then she stuck her finger in a cold cream jar and put her finger up under the sarong, as if she was lubricating herself. She pretended to urinate into a container and threw its contents at the boy and the buffalo. They both tried to avoid it, squealing in disgust. The woman and the boy then pretended to have sex, then they each simulated sex with the buffalo. Next, the buffalo gave each of them mock oral sex.

To know which tale was being enacted and to understand how and why it diverged from the original version requires intimate familiarity with Thai culture, language, and humor. The performances almost always adapted traditional folk tales from various regions of Thailand, passed down through generations of storytelling at home. These tales are often performed at Buddhist temple fairs and other events Thais frequently attend, so the Thai audience is familiar with theses narratives and can easily recognize the alterations. Performed at village fairs, community gatherings and on television, this style of skit/farce mocks traditional stories and gender conventions. The skits performed for a mainstream Thai audience often feature cross-dressing, especially men performing as women, and the actors suffer no condemnation, the audience delighting in the spectacle. Likewise, song and dance performances by *kathoey* in other venues such as the well-known Calypso Cabaret are popular events, well attended by members of Bangkok's upper-middle and middle classes. The performance at DJ Station differed from these other performances by targeting its particular audience, emphatically attacking female sexuality, ridiculing heterosexual acts, and making fun of sex acts between men while clearly privileging them. DJ Station's skits mocked well-known Thai depictions of conventional romance, feminine modesty, heterosexual coupling, and the hierarchies and racism embedded in dominant society, all the while replicating the protocols followed by mainstream revisions of traditional tales. This simultaneous derision and replication of Thai traditions and the expectations of dominant communities reflect and work through the conflicted memberships held by self-identified gay Thai men.

While the Thai audience always laughed and cheered at this segment of the show—clearly their favorite—most non-Thais ignored it, talking to each other or standing at one of the bars. The popularity of the show, which was referred to and laughed about throughout the rest of the evening's dancing and meeting *farang*, suggest that self-identified Thai gay men were not solely looking for and at *farang* in the process of fashioning their identities. Thai men's enthusiasm for the show demonstrates that their interactions with and transformations of mainstream Thai culture are also important factors in their creation of new positions.

The show changed nightly, and most Thais attending enjoyed critiquing each performance. It served as the inauguration of the evening; not many, if any, people danced before it, but after it was finished, the dance floor, center of the club's activity, was packed. In addition, after the show, the Thai men turned their attention to each other and the *farang* present. They stood in groups, danced with each other, but most Thai men focused outward, looking for "cute *farang*." Pointing out whom they liked, they challenged each other to approach the men they admired. Occasionally they made jokes or comments about the show or about each other, but meeting *farang* occupied most of their attention. The prominence of the show provides one more example where self-identified Thai gay men do not simply go looking for and at *farang*. The Thai men's enthusiasm for the show illustrated that their interaction with and transformation of mainstream Thai culture also occupied a central part of their identity construction and/or actions. While watching, laughing, and cheering at the show, Thai men identified with each other and the performers rather than with some form of international community. Through the show, Thai-ness was simultaneously reaffirmed and revised.

While not addressing the *farang* in the club directly, the show occured in a space charged by their presence. For example, while the *farang* were, for the most part, excluded from direct address, the MCs or the performers often acknowledged their existence in both Thai and in English. The *farang*'s location at the back of the club and by the bars meant they saw the Thai audience viewing and interacting with the show. This incorporated the Thai audience into the performance since they were watched (and aware of this) while they watched. As a result, the Thai audience performed for the *farang* audience, emphasizing their reactions and gesturing in ways that some men explained were coded as characteristic of an international gay community—screeching, giggling, and throwing up their hands. Yet they refrained from full participation in this international community by directing their gaze towards the show. Focusing on this revision of Thai culture while aware that they were being watched by *farang*, these men incorporated, revised, and inhabited positions combining mainstream Thai culture with what they perceived as international gay culture in previously unimagined ways.

The performers consisted of self-identified gay Thai men and *kathoey*. During the show, the self-identified gay men dressed in costume, in drag or masculine "as men," while the *kathoey* always performed in feminine clothing, executing extremely stylized, feminine gestures. The Thai audience admired all of the performers, and *kathoey* were recognized as integral, and highly- skilled members of this community activity. Despite their respected participation as performers, *kathoey* were frequently rejected by gay Thai men whom I knew. They ridiculed them and highlighted their differences. In Eric Allyn's introduction of the translated stories in *The Dove Coos: Gay Experiences by The Men of Thailand* he described the position of *kathoeys* in the Thai societal hierarchies as undesirable and ill-fated. "Popularly seen as both a pitiable creature and a fascinating, glamorous anomaly, as a product of bad *kamma* (karma) in a previous life or, in a dated adaptation of Western psychology, as one warped by the lack of a proper male role model" (*The Dove Coos*, 1992, p. 6). In spite of this, *kathoey* in Bangkok have been migrating from working in the sex industry, acting as second class women in predominately female "off-bars" to occupying the spaces, such as bars and cafes, that target non-Thai gay tourists. More likely to find approval among *farang* gay men than with heterosexual customers who might have mistaken them for "real women," they were increasingly attending clubs and bars considered part of the gay community. As their presence augmented over time, the sometimes-violent refusal to recognize *kathoey* membership in the Thai gay community diminished and an increasing proportion of the self-identified gay Thai male population now accepts them. While Thai men who consider themselves gay did not want to be classified as *kathoey*, especially by the mainstream Thai community, some self-identified gay men faced similar problems when constructing an identity based on sexual practices. Members in each of these categories experienced conflicting loyalties because they desired both to be accepted as members of the mainstream Bangkok community and to participate in these fringe communities. In addition, the condemnation and ridicule that self-identified gay men received has waxed and waned, despite being a visible presence in Bangkok in 2014, continue to be conflated with the simultaneously increasing *kathoey* and Trans visibility, and while these populations intersect, these distinctions remain. Successful negotiations leading to mainstream acceptance made by *kathoey* provided models for self-identified gay Thai men in their attempts to situate themselves. Moreover, the increasing participation of *kathoey* in the Bangkok gay community provided opportunities for mutual alliances.[37]

Theoretical descriptions of Thai gayness in English continually untangle this connection between *kathoey* and self-identified Thai gay men. Rosalind Morris has asserted that the sex of *kathoey* is normally considered

---

37 Benedict Anderson provides the following explanation of the role in which class plays how these men identify themselves: "It isn't that *kathoey* have low social standing, but that only people of low social standing are *kathoey*. Class norms are such that effeminate middle class or upper class boys simply aren't permitted to dress in drag on an everyday basis. ... Family status and respectability are at stake. [G]ayness is a middle class thing mainly, or a thing for people aspiring to middle class status. Insofar as *kathoey* equals lower class, you'd see why there might be a wish to stigmatize people too close to you (B. Anderson, personal communication, 1997)..

an alternative—neither male nor female (1994). Assuming that *kathoey* possess this gender even before conception, Allyn's confirmed that there is a general feeling that being a *kathoey* results from misdeeds committed in former lives. In contrast, self-identified gay men actively construct their gayness. Oat declared, "For me, [the idea that one can be born gay] is ridiculous! You are born, and you don't know anything until you learn and explain what you like." (Oat, personal communication, 2004). In *Dear Uncle Go,* Peter Jackson highlighted the contrast between their positions. "Because gayness represents a claim within the order of masculinity in Thailand, its development has had little impact on the low social standing of the *kathoey*. Indeed, Eric Allyn...suggests that the emergence of masculine-identified gayness in Thailand parallels an increasing stigmatization of *kathoeys* in recent years" (Jackson, 1995, pp. 268-9).

While these beliefs show that *kathoey* and gay men do not share circumstances, other discussions, sometimes from identical sources, address the emergence of the gay community in Bangkok by invoking a comparison as a means of explanation. *The Dove Coos* is a translation of Thai erotica published in three Thai language magazines. A popular book, it regularly sold out in the international bookstores of Bangkok and has several volumes of additional stories. In the introduction, Allyn gave men having sex with men in Thailand the following gloss:

> In this Southeast Asian Buddhist kingdom with an eight-hundred-year history and a unique, rich culture, homosexual acts fall into a grey area, marginally addressed by Thai morality and its social institutions. Gay *sex* tends not to be taken seriously and, at worst, it is

thought that one can become habituated to homosexual acts and "addicted" to it. The gay male with a distinct, masculine-identified identity, as Westerners understand, predominates in Thailand, but this idea only recently articulated by Thai gays themselves. The more dominant model is the effeminate male or transvestite (*gathuy*) [sic]. (Allyn, 1995, p. 6)

This introduction separates acts from identities and presents two distinct, non-intersecting categories for Thai gay identity—western style gay and "the more dominant" *kathoey*. Yet one identity is used to explain the position of the other. Since gay identity, "as Westerners understand," is paralleled with *kathoey* in this passage, it receives a different status than non-identifying sex acts that occur between Thai men. The attempts to separate and delineate the differences between the two identities, repeated in the majority of accounts of Thai male-to-male sexual practices, imply a tension. The similarities between these positions call for careful consideration about the ways in which they diverge.

The connection between these two identities also occurs in English-language newspapers. The appearance of articles about gays in other cultures in the *Bangkok Post* and *The Nation*[38] coincided with discussions about the presence of *kathoey* in Thailand. Both kinds of articles involved westerners—the former because of the location of gays, the latter to provide contextualization. I could find no articles about Thai men having sex with men or western gays before 1992, but since

---

38 Interestingly, both these English-language daily newspapers claim a majority Thai readership.

1995, depictions and discussions of men having sex with men, normally termed gay, appear regularly. The increase in these types of articles has been exponential, and the tones and perspectives they reflect are rapidly expanding.

"Outlook," the lifestyle section of the *Bangkok Post*, has run several features about *kathoey* and the attention they receive from Thais. In each article, *farang* provide explanations for their existence. "The Boys who Steal the Show," written by local journalist Malcolm Linton, featured an interview with the German manager and choreographer and descriptions about several of the performers at Calypso Cabaret—a popular venue where *kathoey* performed as women in ornate western style dresses—dancing while lip-synching to mostly western cabaret songs, R'n'B, and occasionally, Thai ballads. The article described the show as family-oriented and immensely popular, the two shows per evening almost always selling out. While many *farang* tourists attended the show, the majority of the audience was Thai. The popularity of the show represents the Thai community's acceptance of *kathoey* as performers. Because *kathoey* exist throughout Thailand, and their presence has been incorporated into mainstream Thai entertainment, it was the skill of the performers as well as their professional costumes that established the Calypso Cabaret performance as family entertainment.

Another article about *kathoey* featured an interview with the leading authority on Thai male sex and gender, Peter Jackson, where the interviewer asked Jackson to describe the Thai fascination with people who possess atypical genitals: "From time to time a hermaphrodite child who is not completely male or female is born, and pictures of the naked babies appear on the front pages of the newspapers. Westerners think this is very unusual, but I think Thais have a fascination with people who are not fully either male or female" (Kanjanawanawan, 1995, p. 31). Jackson also said that he believed many men might have had sex with *kathoey* "before marriage before the practice of hiring sex workers became widespread" (Kanjanawanawan, 1995, p. 31). Centered on Jackson's research rather than actual *farang*, the article functions as an interpretive report by an outsider, targeted for readers who share Jackson's outside status, rather than as a description of a Thai cultural practice explained by Thais for outsiders. This highly mediated perspective, rather than direct reporting, provides distance from the actual information. And Jackson's authoritative position as *farang* researcher heterosexualized men who have sex with *kathoey*, who by *farang* standards would be considered to be participating in homosexual sex acts.

These two articles describe not only the existence of *kathoey* for a considerable amount of time, but, more importantly, their acceptance as members of mainstream Thai society. In each of the examples of *kathoey* featured in the English-language press, a *farang* was interviewed to give their background and history. *Kathoey* were the objects of investigation rather than the subjects. Even the utterances of *kathoey* were paraphrased rather than reported directly. In the first article, written by a *farang*, the German manager was quoted at length, describing the significance of the Cabaret as well as the lives of the *kathoey* dancers both inside and outside of the theater. In the second article, a *kathoey,* a Thai historian, or social scientist could have provided the contextualization of the *kathoey's* place in Thai history and society, but Peter Jackson was interviewed instead. The ideas originating from a *farang* in each case implies a western acceptance of these people; couching the presentation in the words of *farang* helps guide the non-Thai reader's interpretation and softens reactions about subject matter and cultural variances.

Throughout my last interview with Oat, while we discussed what it meant to be gay in Thailand, he contrasted the word "gay" with the word "man" as if a Thai must choose to be one or the other. He also described *kathoey* in opposition to men. When I asked him directly if a gay was not a man, he responded, "I think a man is a man and a gay is a kind of man who has sex with a man and who can love a man." A *kathoey* is "different because they are men who want to be woman. Gay is just a man who wants to be man and is just *like* a man. *Kathoey* wants to be a woman and have everything the body of a woman has" (Oat, personal communication, 2004). Oat's qualification that gays are a "kind of man" rather than a man reveals another site of contradiction encompassed by identifying as gay. Sometimes it was described as an identity, sometimes as participation in the gay community, and sometimes it related directly to having sex with *farang*. Consistently, however, it was positioned with or against *kathoey*. Although the comparisons of being gay with *kathoey* ranged from close correspondence to extremely different, non-coincidental positionings, the continual reference to *kathoey* when discussing being gay in Thailand illustrates that such a relationship exists. The continual slippage between gayness as a western position and *kathoey* as something Thai showed Oat's efforts to describe a position that is neither yet incorporates features of both. The incorporation of English into his lexicon afforded him more ways to articulate this position.

"Sleazy, seedy scenes you'd imagine in some righteous cop movie"[39]

The following section explores some of the depictions of gayness in the English-language press and analyzes how gay Thais constructing eroticized objects and situations alter international gay images. Most of the short stories in *The Dove Coos* series describe men having sex with men, although the men do not classify themselves as gay. Some of these depictions link *farang* or *farang* culture to the erotic situations. Peter Jackson and Eric Allyn have asserted that possibilities for sexual identification are being created by the introduction of western gay culture. Now, they have claimed, Thai men who have sex with men have more ways to articulate their desire for a certain type of masculine gay man (Jackson, 1995, pp. 226-288). *Farang* cultures presented in *The Dove Coos* are eroticized, whether appearing in the form of language, *farang* in Thailand, mapped onto Thai bodies, or implicit in professions involving participation in international markets.

In some of *The Dove Coos'* stories, the presence of English increases

---

39 This quote and the following two excerpts attributed to Joe (name changed) come from a description that he wrote in May 1996 at my request about how his time in Thailand had affected his self-perception. All other references from Joe took place during informal interviews.

the possibilities for expressing pleasure. One story depicts a Thai English-language teacher who, while tutoring a student at his home, initiates a sexual affair. In the opening, it seems the shy student, who stutters and cannot speak a word of English, will prove unteachable. Then the tutor and the student have sex. The writer describes the following scenario:

> "Fuck me faster, harder!" [the student] pleaded. "Please, sir! It feels so good!"
> I was so stunned and excited by his passion that I didn't realize he'd spoken English. "That was the most complete sentence I ever heard you speak, Ek. Where did you learn that kind of talk?"
> "From a magazine called *In Touch* my friend lent me."
> "You understand what you were saying?"
> "Sure, sir. It was the first English I could ever remember."
> That night, he taught me a few more really filthy phrases in English and several things I had not thought about doing. From that night on, after tutoring him in polite English, he taught me a whole encyclopedia of sexology. He also stopped stuttering.
> (Allyn, 1992, pp. 36-7)

In this passage, learning English not only provided the opportunity for sex between teacher and student, it comically reversed the expectations set up in the pupil/teacher dynamic. The shy, stuttering student, unable to understand or speak English, was transformed through sex as a result of his exposure to the combination of English-language teacher and

English-language magazine. The knowledge gleaned from the English magazine enhanced his erotic acumen, enabling him to teach his teacher. And this knowledge and acumen enabled his speech fluency during sex. The story depicted a common Thai scenario, a student being tutored in English, added a series of erotic twists and, in the process, suggested sexual pleasures may accompany English-language learning experiences. Furthermore, the story insinuated that *farang* gay men exercise exotic acts and that the knowledge and practice of these acts increases sexual pleasure.

The expansion of available western media as well as the growing presence of *farang* bodies in Thailand, especially Bangkok, led to increasing numbers of erotic depictions that included *farang*, but in some cases there was a deviation from the standard plot. In "The Sandwich," for example, the Thai protagonist described a *farang* who attracted his attention. "There was a *farang* sitting at the table next to mine. He was strikingly handsome...in his early twenties, with a face and body and style of dress that could easily be a fashion model's. He was like those men in GQ, a men's fashion magazine from America" (Allyn, 1992, p. 29). The *farang*'s stereotypical features, conforming to a generalized notion of western gay culture's aesthetics, were assumed to be erotic, and an American magazine contextualized his appearance. The existence of this magazine in Thailand provides increasing vocabularies for narrating a desirable body. Consequently, this man is depicted as a prototype, possessing no attributes that mark him as more than an anonymous figure, eroticizing a foreign body in a manner similar to the western Orientalist practice of sexualizing stereotyped female Asian bodies. The author's attraction to this body leads, of course, to sex, but in this story he is "sandwiched" between this *farang* and his Thai companion. While self-identified gay Thai men often compete with each other for the attention of gay *farang*, here this does not occur. Instead, the narrator is "surprised to see the Thai standing there smiling" and invited him along instead of "start[ing] a fight over him" (Allyn, 1992, p. 30). After the *farang* returns to France, the relationship continues between the two Thai men. Thus the standard erotic scenario shifts and mutual desire for a *farang* body provides the impetus for a relationship between two Thai men.

Joe, who lived in Thailand from 1993-1997, described his initiation into the upscale, flourishing gay sites:

> One day Law invited me to go shopping at Chatuchak Park, a huge weekend market. ... On the way home, Law suggested that we go to Babylon. "I didn't bring any gym clothes." "It doesn't matter. Everyone just wears a towel." I, as well as Oat, had never been to a gay sauna before and both expected the sleazy, seedy scenes you'd imagine in some righteous cop movie. The place was impeccably clean, elegant, equipped with a super gym and served great food. That was my first trip to Babylon and my first of many workouts. (Joe, personal communication, 1996)

Joe had never been involved in a gay community in the United States, so while his initiation to this international gay community came from his position as a *farang*, it was mediated by the experience and expertise of his gay Thai friend, Law. In addition, his Thai boyfriend, Oat, was also becoming involved with this community. The two compared their expectations and beliefs as each positioned themselves according to what they understood the scene to be. Tom's surprise to find his expectations of "sleaze" dashed reflects western heterosexual assumptions about western gay saunas and gyms. His expectations were dashed not because the place was located in the Far East and thus different from a scene in a "righteous cop movie," but because the place turned out to be a clean, modern, international style gym with good *farang* food. His years of participation in Bangkok's booming society have changed his generalizations—he no longer assumed that what he does not know will be "exotically eastern," but, as one outside of any gay scene, expected gay sites to embody western non-gay stereotyped depictions. Instead the sauna, similar to other gay gyms throughout the world, reflected Bangkok's adoption and adaptation of *farang* communities, their practices, and accoutrements.

One result of having an international gay scene in Bangkok was its focus on the white male body as the primary object of desire. This image was privileged at DJ Station and other bars, saunas, and meeting places. Gay Thai men constantly described their ideal partners to me according to this standard. Once, at a dinner party, twelve different Thai men described almost precisely the same attributes for their ideal partner: "white, with a large chest and tight abdominals, short hair, clean, and well dressed. And rich."[40]

African American gay author and poet Keith Boykin has written in his memoir *One More River To Cross*, "Like its heterosexual

_____

40 This was literally what two of the men described together while laughing and acting as if they were embarrassed.

counterpart, the white gay media usually projects Eurocentric images of beauty that transmit messages of inferiority to blacks and others who do not fit into the white stereotype" (1996, p. 216). Similarly, Thai and *farang* media, as well as other sources of information, present a particular body that is the archetype for desire, and predominately this body is young, white, male, and fit. Law admitted that his desire changed based on international gay standards, but he attributed this to having better sex. "I have more feelings when I have sex with *farang*. Though it depends on how they look. … Thai male bodies, the way they are proportioned, are not attractive to me" (Law, personal communication, 1996).

Often, self-identified gay Thai men in Bangkok's gay community followed this prescription for desire. Joe has acknowledged, accepted, and conformed to what he interprets as a partner's expectations. He asserted that Jin encouraged him to attain this body type:

> "I think you have a worm, Joe." Jin said, laying around on the bed on a hot April afternoon, the peak of hot season. "You're too thin. Look like a ghost. Mr. Bones."

> Jin, when not commenting on my skinny body was continually trying to get me to fatten up. He was studying cooking at the Oriental Hotel and liked to show off his knowledge of well-balanced meals and good nutritional habits. And he always paid for the meals after sex.

> It's not that I wasn't healthy or even in shape. Despite the Bangkok heat and hot season humidity, I was running ten kilometers, three or four times a week in a nearby

park, and figured out a way to use my staircase as an incline for sit- ups and my stomach was tight. I just didn't have the beefy, boyish body Jin fantasized about. So he tried to get at me by trying to convince me that I was sick, had a parasite or something or other. Skinny malnourished guys looked like the locals from his village, a silk producing community outside of Khon Khean, which was the closest I've even come to having a worm by eating a silk worm to appease one of his relatives. IevenwenttothedoctorforacompletecheckuphadanAIDS test and everything just to show Jin I was in top condition. (Joe, personal communication, 1996)

Joe's description of Jin conformed to the stereotype about Thai gay men—the upcountry-boy-made-good-in-Bangkok. Consequently, he assumed that Jin has the same fantasies that these men "should" have because of their participation in the international gay scene. He believed that Jin fantasized about "beefy boyish bod[ies]." The way he could prove to Jin that he was not "Mr. Bones" was through western medicine—a complete checkup by a doctor who utilizes advanced western testing procedures and apparatuses was Joe's attempt to prove to Jin he was in good health and should thus be considered desirable. Joe's description illustrates how how his participation in the Bangkok gay community affected his self-perception. Shortly after this affair ended, Joe began to work out at Babylon, the gym he visited with Law, regularly. He lifted weights to develop his chest, which was met with vociferous approval from his Thai friends. The passage also illustrated that even Joe, who had lived in Bangkok for four years, still projected onto Jin stereotypical desires that conform to the international gay body. As my discussion shows, each of these men had individuated strategies for identification and unique conceptions concerning their membership in the Thai gay community of Bangkok. Thus their desires may vary analogously to the way they positioned and constructed themselves.

While the white gay male body often held a privileged aesthetic position in Bangkok's economies of desire, this situation was sometimes more complicated. For example, Thai bodies can be eroticized by taking on a western athletic appearance. The following translation of an anonymous story from *Midway Magazine* in *The Dove Coos* alters this stereotype. This story relates the following description of a Thai man dressed in a sexy way: "I wore a sleeveless athletic t-shirt, sport shorts of a thin fabric that gave eyes a tease as it fluttered over my equipment, and sneakers, without socks. I dress like this because I intended to jog at the nearby park after the movie" (Allyn, 1992, p. 19). All of the clothing described is western in its style, invoking a stereotypical *farang* look. Not only does the author equate sexy with a western sports style unacceptable by Thai standards—a sleeveless T-shirt and thin sport shorts is considered inappropriate and improper to wear out in a small Thai town—he also adopts a western lifestyle, stating that he will go jogging afterward. This activity is not usually considered a sport for Thais though it is gaining some popularity.

The following depiction of a Thai man appeared in the short story "Chinese Battle Strategy Defeats the Dragon" by Wan in *The Dove Coos*:

He was very good-looking, and dressed sexy in a tank-top and tight cotton running shorts…the tall young man had a build that was made from disciplined training. He had broad shoulders, arms that revealed the thick sinews of muscle when he flexed, a chest that strained his tank top, and a slim waist atop beefy thighs. (1992, pp. 50-1)

His tight clothing and muscular build resembles a stereotypical gay white man, contrasting with most Thai models in Thai gay magazines who are normally young, slender, and boyish rather than beefy. By projecting various western erotic stereotypes on a Thai body, Thai men produce new sexualized depictions of Thai men for Thai men (originally). The range of erotic possibilities is further enhanced when it is revealed that the body is that of a Thai banker. Working in a bank, as the editors of the anthology described, became sexy with Thailand's economic boom. "The standard for male attractiveness among Thai gay men is the muscular, athletic type in his twenties. … It is only recently that the businessman has become an erotic ideal, reflecting a shift in his status in Thai society" (Allyn, 1992, p. 13). The prestige accorded to financial success by capitalist cultures accompanies participation in international economies, and desire circulates around these new sites of status. While interactions with international markets have increased the possibilities for gay Thai men to imagine, eroticize, and desire, *farang*, too, have access to these representations of gay culture produced by Thais.

Despite the proliferation of English-language depictions of men having sex with men as well as the growing number of sexualized images, the objects of desire are still strictly coded in the Bangkok scene, and gay men can and do fall into prescribed positions. White men, like Joe, can take advantage of their whiteness and try to construct their bodies in order to conform to this code. However, non-whites may automatically fall outside the categories of desire. In the U.S., Asian males are frequently represented as impotent, naïve, and unthreatening. International film maker and critic Richard Fung has explained, "Asians…are collectively seen as undersexed" (1991, p. 146). This Eurocentric generalization also has affected the Bangkok scene. As a result, many Thai men tried to build and sculpt their bodies following these codes. Law introduced Joe to this gay sauna where the majority of the men were Thai. Simultaneously, Thai men responded to the stereotypes projected upon them by *farang* gay men. Oat described some of the expectations that he perceived coming from white gay men:

> I have known so many westerners who are gay, and they came to Thailand just to find a lover. They want to find a lover that will be with them for the rest of their life. But they come here to Thailand, and they use their imagination and think that Thai boys are sweet or whatever. But I think eventually they see it's not true. I don't think it's easy to find that type of good Thai gay man. Most of them just want money from westerners. (Oat, personal communication, 2004)

Oat has said that Thai men involved with *farang* try to occupy this imaginary position, but, after a while, they normally fail to conform to the *farang*'s preconceived image. At this point, relationships often flounder. Disappointed but not disillusioned, *farang* men frequently found new Thai partners and uncritically reasserted their stereotypical expectations.

The constructions of these newly imagined positions, identities, and practices in Bangkok continue to be in flux. Established practices such as "The Show" at DJ Station frequently changed, disrupting established routines and encouraging reevaluations of expectations. For example, on Halloween 1995, DJ Station decorated with silver from floor to ceiling, calling the evening "A Touch of Silver." About twenty Thai men and one farang expatriate donned elaborate costumes; some cross-dressed while others resembled exotic birds or futuristic robots.

Image 2.1

On this night, the costumed guests became the show. The two MCs called them onto the stage. Most of the men in the club approached the stage to watch the proceedings, and farang constituted much of the audience. While the MCs interviewed the Thai men about their costumes in English, they only spoke Thai to the farang contestant, who acted as if he could not understand and encouraged teasing from the MCs and the audience. The posturing of this farang, a long time member of this scene, created an opportunity for Thai men to ridicule rather than show respect or sexual interest—the most frequent manners of interaction. The ways in which the men of the self-identified gay community in Bangkok describe themselves and present their sexualities augment and change in response to their sense of the community, which is becoming larger, more diverse, and more established. Since this study, the Thai economy has shifted dramatically and many previous economic practices and expectations have been reassessed and reformulated. These changing circumstances mark new opportunities, constraints, and factors to consider. Charting these trends and documenting the various articulations provides increased possibilities—both for imaging oneself and understanding others. If, as Law prosed, being gay enabled him to change things, examining what constitutes these changes, whether imbibed or enacted, provides the means to understanding and critiquing the position of self-identified gay Thai men in Bangkok.

3

"Women Who Follow Non-Conformist Ways": Thai Women Loving Women

Anjaree was the first Thai organization specifically targeting women without a gendered, inequities-based agenda. Headquartered in Bangkok, it had members throughout Thailand, providing information, encouraging community formation and sponsoring social events for Thai women-who-love-women. In Thai, *Anjaree* means "women who follow non-conformist ways." Despite the organization's entrenchment—it existed for over a decade and boasts a membership of over six hundred— its founder, spokesperson, and leader, Anjana Suvarnananda complained that she was at a loss for words, both in Thai and in English, to adequately describe her identity as a woman-who-loves-women following non-conformist ways. At the Sixth International Conference for Thai Studies, she presented a new Thai word that she had created—*yingrakying*—

that she hoped would circulate as a new word for women "who have erotic feelings or love feelings for other women" ("Lesbianism," 1996). While Suvarnananda often used the word "lesbian" to describe herself and members of her organization to *farang*, she avoided the term when describing the site-specific community in Thailand. In addition, when speaking in Thai and to Thai people, she resisted using the word lesbian. Though widely understood, many Thais, including those involved in women centered relationships, considered it vulgar and derogatory. When talking to Thais, Suvarnananda employed and revised the commonly used Thai words for women-who-love-women. Rather than perpetuating the use of these established terms and the stereotypes that accompany them, Suvarnananda addressed the changing situations of Thai women-who-love-women. At this meeting she stated, "We are not sure if this [new] term will go down well or if this will be the term we stick to or not. We are in the process of building our own culture and terminologies" (Suvarnananda, "Lesbianism," 1996).

The new word reflected Suvarnananda's education at Hague, access to western ideas, and fluency in English. Because of these extensive experiences she did not want to simply invoke English but, instead, deployed her knowledge to affect community formation and adaptation, broadening the community's way of conceptualizing itself and its individual members. *Yingrakying* literally means "woman-loves-woman" or "women-love-women" in Thai, originating from the terminology currently *en vogue* with western women-centered organizers and academics—"women who love women." Rather than adopting the English word and using it in Thai in the manner the word lesbian was employed, Suvarnananda reformulated this phrase in order to match her own intentions through translation and transformation.[41] In this case, knowledge of the English language and *farang* ideas become tools rather than models for linguistic community formation. Her word becomes a tactical means for interaction and community building that encouraged altering the way women imagined themselves according to changing circumstances.

This chapter examines the shifting positions of women in Bangkok over the past decade as a result of increasing opportunities for education and financial stability. It presents varied and conflicting accounts by *yingrakying* that delineate what constituted previous positions, and then shows how Suvarnananda and *Anjaree* posit alternatives throughout the creation of words and communities. The challenges faced by Thai women-who-love-women when speaking about sexuality both inside and outside of *Anjaree* are also considered. To this end, I examine the Bangkok-based English language magazine *Pink Ink*, which featured a column between 1997 and 1998 about women who love women. Over the last several decades, these non-heterosexually conforming women have emerged from historically geographic and sexual margins to a place of visibility in Bangkok.

Anjaree's function as a social club where women could meet

---

41 When discussing the women of *Anjaree*, I will henceforth utilize Suvarnananda's term. However, when discussing Thai women who love women in general, I will use women loving women. While loving is not a particularly apt word, lesbian is not a reasonable alternative. Women loving women is particularly problematic as its often paired paired with MSM (men who have sex with men). These terms reflect an astounding gender bias--men in same sex relationships have sex while women possess love. These increasingly acceptable terms perpetuate this gendered dichotomy.

women provided the impetus for my increasing involvement during my tenure of research in Bangkok. The Thai women-who-loved-women that I knew that were not members of *Anjaree* were either friends from my previous stay in Thailand or friends of friends. I conducted interviews in May, June, and October 1996. In addition, some of the examples cited occurred while socializing during the eight months previous to my decision to consider these interactions part of my research. I employed more formal procedures, acquiring most of my information through interviews that took place, for the most part, in English. Privileging English for the interview processes encouraged the women to speak about identity and sexuality in ways that would not occur in a Thai-language setting. It also highlights the effects of the English language on their identity construction and self-representation.

The position of *yingrakying* in Thailand has changed concurrently with the rest of Thai society as a result of the economic boom, particularly in Bangkok, over the last decade. One societal custom that conformed to the increasing need for educated, middle-class expertise was women's participation in business. In addition to managing family finances, Thai women have often been entrepreneurs and salespeople. In accordance with previous Thai practices, women often fill the increasing demand for economic expertise. In the past decade, many women have entered the middle-class workforce, enjoying the increasing opportunities for education and individual economic security. As a result, marriage—the Thai presses repeatedly report—is no longer the primary concern of women in their twenties and thirties. Many women are opting for career success, job stability, and comfortable salaries before marriage and motherhood. Middle-class women—single, in their twenties and thirties, economically independent and educated—make up a large and visible part of the population of *yingrakying* and other Thai women-who-love-women.

Tom and Dee

Fifty years ago, there was a law in Thailand that forbade women to have sex with other women. The legislation appeared in response to the spread of western discussions about perversion. However, currently the most common words to describe Thai women-who-love-women—Tom and Dee—appeared ten years before the law was deleted. Suvarnananda, who frequently mentions this antiquated law in her discussions of *yingrakying*, does not know whether the Thai government did not notice the existence of the words and identities of Tom and Dee, or if this was a strategy to deny the increasingly visible existence of Toms (Suvarnananda, 1995).

Young women in Thailand who live with their families rarely occupy a sexualized position. Female friends often spend large amounts of time together including passing the night in each other's beds, and the display of emotional intimacy may not lead family members to suspect sexual activity. In *Toms and Dees: Transgender Identity and Female Same-Sex Relationships in Thailand* (2004), Megan Sinnott discusses the position of female friendships and women's sexuality in contemporary Thailand and provides extended interviews from women identifying as Tom or Dee. In my own interviews, one woman recounted that her mother found out through a friend that she was involved with a woman. Despite the mother's disapproval about the relationship and her request that it be terminated, she did not admonish the daughter for continuing to invite her girlfriend to her bedroom to spend the night. Sharing a bed did not offend her mother, the daughter reports, because the relationship was not sexualized in her mother's imagination. This same mother would object to a man merely entering her daughter's bedroom. As Sinnott's extensive ethnography revealed, between women there exists a type of invisibility in plain sight.

The word Tom comes from the English word "tomboy" and Dee from the word "lady." These terms coincide with the terms butch and femme, respectively, when referring to lesbian positionings; however, they are neither mere imitations of their English derivatives nor American descriptions of butch/femme dynamics.[42] The use of words derived from English to name these distinctly Thai identities conforms to the Thai habit of adopting English words where no Thai word exists. For example, in the nineteenth century, when a couple was involved romantically, they would declare themselves married. No registration was required, but marriage was premised on a man's financial commitment in return for a woman's commitment to run a household and remaining sexually faithful. Over time, having "boyfriends" and "girlfriends" became a possible social relationship that acknowledged interest yet did not entail specific commitments, and a new word emerged. The Thai word is *faen*— derived either from the English word "friend" or "fan." The meaning for

---

42 See Sue Ellen Case's "The Butch-Femme Aesthetic" (1993) and Joan Nestle's *That Persistent Desire: A Femme Butch Aesthetic* (1992).

this Thai word, however, does not directly reflect either English referent. Rather, it named a situation occurring in Thailand that did not yet have a term to describe it. Similarly, the Thai word *farang* comes from the French word "francais," yet the Thai use the word *farang* to refer to most non-Asians, especially Europeans and Americans. The same practice of linguistic adaptation took place when the words Tom and Dee entered the language; they do not directly reflect their English origins but instead mark the noticeable presence of a new position in Thai society. English provides a source for words to describe previously unnamed positions or circumstances. Like the word gay that I discussed in the previous chapter, these words are significantly altered in the process of cultural translation, yet they still retain traces of their original meanings.

Farang gender models, educational systems, and city infrastructures have a history of being interpreted by Thai rulers and mandated for the Thai populace. Historian David Wyatt describes some of the mandates of King Vajiravudh, explaining how they reflected what he saw as strategies for Thai modernity during his sojourn in the west:

> One of the most persistent themes in [King Vajiravudh's] writings might be termed modernity—that is, encouraging, even exhorting, people to act and live as modern people did in the West. He introduced surnames and coined names for hundreds of families; he refashioned the flag of Siam…he introduced the first national holidays…he promoted team sports, particularly soccer football; he worked to improve the status of women by encouraging them to mix socially with men and by arguing

for monogamy in place of widespread Siamese polygamy;
and he was an ardent supporter of modern education.
(Wyatt, 1984, p. 228)

The king coined surnames, yet he did not require Thais to become Smiths or Jones. Similarly, the national holidays reflected Thailand's commemoration of their kings by celebrating the day they died rather than, following western practices, celebrating leaders' birthdays. One reason he encouraged monogamy was his disinterest in women. Previous kings supported a harem, where families could gain honor and prestige by "donating" a beautiful daughter. This king ignored this practice, taking no wives at all and creating a court consisting only of men.[43] "Modernity," according to Wyatt, is the way King Vajiravudh promoted his adaptations of western practices for Thailand.

After the military coup that toppled the absolute monarchy (the king who followed Vajiravudh was young and held the title for only a short time) on 24 June 1932, the government continued to promote "modernity," and "Thai ideals" were still defined in dialogue with European practices. As a result of the complete shift in the way in which the government was set up (Thailand had heretofore been a kingdom or system of kingdoms), nationalism, and masculinity were redefined for Thai citizens. Rosalind Morris maintains that the reason Thai husbands were instructed to kiss their wives before work was a way

---

43 The public knowledge and acceptance of King Vajiravudh's homoerotic desire by the Thai population both then and now illustrates how sexual actions do not necessarily infer sexual identities and homosexual actions are not categorically perceived as negative in Thai culture. See my previous chapter for a full consideration of these beliefs.

to enforce what she non-specifically terms masculinity. "If sexual practice remained invisible to the state—or, rather, if the realm of state visibility excluded erotic relations—the performance of masculinity by men was nonetheless demanded by cultural policies such as those that required men to wear hats and ties or to kiss their wives before leaving for work" (Morris, 1997, p. 58). However, promotion of these practices more likely served as a marker of the new government's success at achieving modernity. In Kukrit Pramoj's well known novel, *Si Phaendin*, Ploi and her husband express amazed discomfort at these rituals, yet despite their secure positions in society and their respectable age, they perform these new rituals in order to help the country.[44]

Serving a similar function, Tom and Dee positions can contribute to describing masculinity and femininity in a manner that is in dialogue with *farang* conceptions. The positions of Tom and Dee neither replicate/imitate western butch/femme constructions nor do they exist entirely in isolation from western forms of desire and societal positioning. The presence of intermediary or mutated positions is often overlooked in scholarship about gender and sexuality in non-western cultures.[45] Recognizing this, Anthropologist Will Roscoe critiqued pervious scholarship that described the Zuni tribe of Native Americans as "gay." Roscoe noted that the term "gay" simplifies the depiction of

---

44 See Chapter Two for a more about Kukrit Pramoj's *Four Reigns*.

45 Two essays by Dennis Altman, "Global Gaze/Global Gays" (1997) and "Rupture or Continuity?" (1996), are strong examples that work against this practice, attempting to analyze specific details about non-heterosexuality in several Asian countries. See also Ana Maria Alonso and Maria Teresa Koreck's essay, "Silences," which explains how "the use of the terms 'homosexuality,' 'bisexuality,' and 'heterosexuality' with reference to Mexico is rather misleading. . ." (1993, p. 115).

Zuni genders instead of analyzing the ways in which they do not conform to a male/female binary, "Underlying these statements are assumptions about cultural change based on an either/or opposition of 'traditional' and 'assimilated'" (Roscoe, 1995, p. 194). Rather than viewing Tom and Dee in this either/or framework, I will delineate many of its perceived parameters and particularities. Not only are the many kinds of same-sex relationships between women in Bangkok not contained by the terms Tom and Dee, the qualifications and definitions provided by the women I interviewed about what constitutes being Tom and Dee contrast and contradict rather than form a consistent portrayal.

Suvarnananda's attempt to coin a new word follows this Thai pattern of adaptation. As Russian semiotician Mikhail Bakhtin has described in his work on the philosophy of language, words carry traces from their pasts and incorporate the changing histories of the use they receive. "Language, for the individual consciousness, lies on the borderline between oneself and the other. The word in language is half someone else's. It becomes 'one's own' only when the speaker populates it with his own intention, his own accent, when he appropriates the word, adapting it to his own semantic and expressive intention" (Bakhtin, 1981, p. 23). Consequently, the words Tom and Dee are significantly altered in the process of cultural translation, yet they still retain traces of their original meanings. Furthermore, as Megan Sinnott's extensive study, *Toms and Dees*, illustrates through numerous interviews and extensive research (2004), the meanings of Tom and Dee are constantly negotiated by the speaker and the context. And *yingrakying* resonates differently in Thai than "women-loving-women" does in English: these terms have not been strung together before and consequently do not directly reflect the people and organizations that promote equal rights and acceptance for women loving women. Instead, this past is translated and the history changes.

Although the explanations about what designates Tom and Dee dissent, certain patterns emerge. For example, fashion is the most frequently cited indicator of Toms. Men's style shoes, flip-flops or sandals on their feet, Toms wear large polo or oxford cloth shirts tucked into loose jeans of assorted colors. Their hair is short, straight, and styled in a manner that does not require curling or drying when wet. Toms do not carry handbags or purses, but they do wear mobile phones and pagers, which signal their middle-class status, as well as car keys hanging from their belt loops or pockets, a practice otherwise reserved for Thai men. Under their shirts, they wear undershirts instead of bras, and they tend to keep their shoulders hunched slightly forward so as to diminish the visibility of their breasts. Despite what seem to be clearly coded visual clues signaling class stratified positions and realigning gendered practices, however, the Thais I interviewed did not always cite appearance when asked to describe Toms. Conformity to a style of dress or appearance may be provided as attributes signifying Toms, but they do not do so conclusively.

"Active" is another consistent adjective evoked in relation to Toms. When asked to define Tom and Dee, Pari, a *yingrakying* who previously considered herself a Tom, said that a Tom usually takes the "active" role during sex and "does not let another woman see her body or her breasts or whatever." Hiding their bodies, even during sex, "they wear tank tops [as opposed to bras or nothing]; they are active," she stated (Pari, personal communication, 1996). Susan, an American researching gender in Thai politics, has had several relationships with Thai women and reported that mainstream Thai society thinks, "If you're seen as a Tom, that defines your sex in a certain way" (personal communication, 1996). She believes that there is a stereotypical set of assumptions that a general member of Thai society—if they attempted to sexualize the position—would assume, including that "this person would be active in bed" (Susan, personal communication, 1996).[46] Carol, another scholar living in Bangkok and spoke Thai, understood that, "people associate Toms with sexuality. It has a clear sexual meaning to the outside" (personal communication, 1996). For her, coding oneself as Tom through appearance was not merely a fashion statement or dislike for gender conventions; it marked one sexually. However, she also found that the active role of Toms is not limited to sex acts; Toms were also active by controlling the emotional tenor of the relationship, "how intense things are, how emotional things get" (Carol, personal communication, 1996). This has occurred in her own relationships with Toms as well as in other relationships she has observed. While not necessarily the initiators of relationships, Toms are described as

---

46 This particular definition of Tom coincides with the western position of stone butch, a masculine lesbian who refuses direct genital stimulation. Halberstam argues that stone butches "felt compromised being made love to as a woman" but still used other methods to derive sexual pleasure (1998, p. 125). Their existence, she argues, "complicates immensely the imitation hypothesis--or at least the idea that butches are bad copies of men--and codifies at least one register of difference between some general notion of male sexual roles and butch sexual roles" (1998, p. 124). Toms, whether they allow themselves to be touched or not, perform a similar function for Thai understandings of gender, but these understandings are currently in flux as a result of the import of many ideas and customs in the process of globalization.

active in controlling the sex, emotional tenor, and level of commitment.

Several Thai women agree that Toms are "active," yet resist the extension that being Tom includes a sexualized component. They insist that young women who live with their families are rarely imagined as sexual beings unless they involved with a man. Imitating men is also frequently described as an aspect of being Tom. Pari described her former position of Tom as one that imitates a man. Another Tom, Pui, who is college educated, in her thirties, living in Bangkok and financially independent, sells medical textbooks to colleges and doctors and spends most of her time with Thai women in her work and social life. She gives the following definition for Tom:

> [A] woman who loves to see herself and tell herself she is a man is Tom. . . . A Tom will not accept herself as a woman although the truth is, and then she can't be a man too but she has to be somebody, so Tom is what she can be. Tom copy man's rule because she thinks she is, so they act like a man in almost everything—love pretty women, sexy or lady; always say 'pom' [I, masc. sing] and 'krab,' [masculine tag to denote politeness], short hair, men's clothes. (Pui, personal communication, 1997)

Refusing to follow the roles prescribed for women, and wishing, but unable, to be a man, marks the position of Tom for Pui. Yet a Tom is "somebody"—a gender that she can possess—not just a male impersonation or an imperfect woman.[47] Despite this, she still "copies"

---

47 Thus Toms embody Thai female masculinity. Halberstam similarly argues that tomboys, lesbians, butch women and drag kings are not imitations

and "acts like a man." While some Toms describe themselves as better able to provide for the women they love than Thai men, Pui clearly does not imagine her position as superior. Consequently, her relationships tend to be with Dees that are married or engaged; she expects to take second place and eventually be deserted. The desire to be a man is the extreme position for a Tom, one that many women without a large Tom community most often describe.

Having sex or girlfriends are also not defining features of being Tom. Throughout Thailand, the women I interviewed concurred: Toms are not designated by Dee companionship. In fact, Toms frequently form their own communities and networks of friendships without including Dees. Carol stresses community identification rather than sexual actions. "Toms are in a community together, and it extends to their sexual life" and not the other way around (Carol, personal communication, 1996). While community formation is also not a requirement for being Tom, Toms often form social groups ranging in size from two to six or seven. These groups spend their free time together—in restaurants, bars, or taking weekend trips. My informants consistently mentioned Toms they knew that had no girlfriends. Most of these women socialized with other Toms; however, other Toms focused on their relationships with Dees and spent their time with their girlfriends. Frequently Dees that are girlfriends are included in the social events. However, it is rare that a Dee not involved with a Tom remains a part of the social group.

of men but alternative masculinities: "far from being an imitation of maleness, female masculinity actually affords us a glimpse of how masculinity is constructed as masculinity" (*Female Masculinity*, 1998, p. 1).

These Tom communities are often premised on an unspoken agreement not to discuss positions or desires. For example, one group of Toms that I encountered, only one of whom is a member of *Anjaree*, had never discussed whether or not they were Toms before I began associating with them. They all dressed accordingly and looked the part, socializing with each other, but never overtly discussing their own desires. One woman who belonged to this group was a member of *Anjaree*, and she had asked me not to reveal her participation to the others. When I later asked her why, she said she was not sure they were Tom, even though, several years before, three of them had both pursued the same Dee. For some reason, she did not make the assumption, despite the visual clues and their shared object of desire. Yet Toms often speculate about the existence of other Toms. A frequent topic of conversation was whether someone is a Tom or not, though the question was almost never directed at its subject. For example, at restaurants my friends frequently would speculate whether servers were Toms. Despite hair, clothes, and mannerisms that are stereotypically Tom, the conversation kept returning to speculation. "I think she's a Tom. Do you? Yes, I definitely think she's Tom" (Pui, personal communication,.1997). A lot of attention goes to classifying strangers, yet conclusions are rarely drawn, and questions are not asked, even among friends. Community formation is thus often premised on silence about desire and identification among members, displacing self-revelation through assertions about those outside the circle.

When a woman is involved with a Tom, she is considered to be a Dee. But this is neither a permanent, nor fixed, position. A Dee conforms to the mainstream image of Thai femininity and, in fact, any woman in Thailand could be Dee. Dee are often involved with men as well. In fact, it is assumed most Dees will eventually get married and have children, as the position of matriarch is the most powerful and desirable for a Thai woman. A Dee takes the "woman's role" in the relationship following a code for dress, manner, and gestures, and nurturing. During sex, "Dees lay back and enjoy. They cuddle and things. Making love is only one way" (Pui, personal communication, 1997). Passivity during sex is not necessarily the "woman's role" in heterosexual relationships, yet it is premised in the Tom/Dee scenario, partially because of the position of Toms as active and partially because many Toms refuse to expose their bodies, wishing not to reveal feminine attributes. Dees' passivity is described in these terms by all the women with whom I came into contact.[48]

In heterosexual Thai society, men normally initiate contact. However, in Susan's experience with the Tom/Dee scenario, it's acceptable for a Dee to be more flirty. In fact, since Dees are not visually coded, any woman could be fair game to a Tom, so initial contact is often left to Dees. According to Suvarnananda, there are no established symbols that "allow erotic messages and interactions between people," such as pink triangles or rainbow colors. This may account for the acceptability of their initiations. "A Tom is like a moving target. Dees can identify you" (Suvarnananda, personal communication, 1996). These initial

48 See Sinnott's study (2004) for her thorough investigation and theorization of the precariousness of Dee-identity, which she argues is structurally reliant upon a a Tom partner. This follows much theory concerning Butch/Femme dynamics where being Butch is privileged as a realignment of gender and a form of subversion in a way the Femme is not (Butler, Halberstam, and earlier gender theorists). Joan Nestle is one of many who complains about this tendency.

contacts can occur in locations where Toms and Dees are known to frequent, but they also take place in the workplace or at any number of locales where people mix. Thus this acknowledgement that Dees initiate contact contradicts the insistence that Toms cannot be identified by appearance. If Dees approach Toms, they are making assumptions about Tom sexuality based on visual codes. Dees are considered even less visible than Toms marked only, according to some, by their accompaniment of Tom partners. Because their identity is not considered fixed or primary, community formation is even more difficult than for Toms. Carol remarked that she has only seen community formation among Dees at *Anjaree* functions. Pari, Mao, and other women I interviewed pointed out that some Dees are entrenched in traditional family relationships. "Someone married, has kids, decides I've just fallen in love with a Tom" (Pari, personal communication,1996). In these instances, Toms normally spend a lot of time with the entire family, including the husband. They may take the kids out, be included on family trips, and become involved in many of the family's activities. In most cases, the presence of a Tom does not cause suspicions or jealousy, because, as I have suggested, these relationships may not be marked as sexual.

Although *Anjaree* members frequently cite the organization's unique position in the realigning of identities, Tom and Dee positions are transformed by women outside of *Anjaree* as well. Pari stated that many other women do not fit into the Tom/Dee scenario, calling these women "another category" of "people who don't necessarily have to put the role on themselves. ... I know other Thai women who have this feeling of another category. Some of them don't label themselves as lesbians, they just have relationships with women." According to Pari, most of these women have had some type of contact with Europe or the United States—through study, travel, or work. They are also older, normally in their thirties, "They know who they are and don't need to act out anymore," she explained. (Pari, personal communication, 1996).

During a conversation in Thai with a group of Toms and Dees who were not members of *Anjaree,* Carol asked a member of the group who was dressed in men's clothes if she was a Tom or a Dee. She replied, "I'm 60% Dee and 40% Tom because I'm a little bit lazy. I like to get it more than I like to give it." Carol recounted their surprise: "They were just shocked. One woman said, 'I can't believe you said that, no Thai would ever say that. We all think that, but no one would actually say it.'" According to Carol, another Tom present announced, "I can be a Tom or a Dee, too." She seemed attracted to the idea that it would be possible to express that, but I don't think she felt comfortable saying that to her Thai friends (Carol, personal communication, 1996). But some Toms do actually become Dees, and vice versa. Carol also recounted an incident where a Tom she met showed her a picture of a very feminine woman. This photograph, the Tom explained, was taken of her several years before. This woman bragged about her ability to change poles, moving from Dee to Tom in the course of a year. Therefore Tom and Dee positions are not permanently marked on the body; they can be worn and exchanged in some instances. These interchanges described by Carol illustrate that *Anjaree* members are not unique in their efforts to rethink their positions, although in each case the switch is made from one extreme to the other. Because these changes require reimagining and realigning oneself vis-á-vis one's friends, family, and communities, the process is facilitated by the presence of others who are similarly reconfiguring themselves.

Overall, Toms are not defined by their actions, communities, or desires. They are Toms because of the way they look; yet there is no absolute determining marker. Even a Tom cannot be sure that another woman is a Tom. Yet there is a fascination in discovering this, among women in both this community and in mainstream Thai society. Dees, on the other hand, are defined by their relations to Toms. Any woman can be a Dee, as long as she is with a Tom. Without a Tom, her position is not secure. Toms together are imaginable, although their positions must eventually shift, but not Dees.[49] While Toms are described as active, they cannot always control the tenor of the relationship because Dees usually initiate and some may have other partners outside of this dynamic—whether boyfriends, potential boyfriends, or husbands—to consider. In an interview about *Anjaree*, Amporn Boontan explained the pressure to identify as Tom or Dee in Thailand:

> Actually, there are two pressures. The first is, you want
> to find a partner, so you have to identify yourself. When
> I have long hair, people are not sure if I am lesbian, so it
> is hard to meet people like that. But when I had shorter
> hair, then if women were interested, they would already
> know that I like women. And then there is pressure
> from those around you to copy the heterosexual model.

---

49 Sinnott provides the most nuanced study of this positioning of Dees vis-à-vis Toms (2004).

That is, one has to be the leader, and one has to be the follower. And you have to identify yourself as tom or dee in the lesbian community so we can know where you fit. Especially many older lesbian couples, they expect this. If a lesbian couple doesn't fit into this pattern, they will be confused, or think those people aren't real lesbians. So there is pressure from society. It tells us that the man will be with the woman-even if you are homosexual! So you have to copy that role, that one has to be the man and one has to have the woman's role. (Mazner, 1998)

As the *Anjaree* local representative from Chiang Mai, the second largest city, Amporn was well versed in the politics from both within and outside the Tom-Dee configurations in Thailand. She used western terms such as lesbian and homosexual to describe this population, but still found pressure to conform to these dynamics. The ambiguous and conflicting descriptions that I have outlined do not form a coherent picture: Toms are seen but not seen, sexually marked but invisible; and Dees can exist without Toms but they initiate contact with active, yet inconclusively visible Toms.

"Nonconformist Ways"

Lek, an *Anjaree* member and organizer, one of the first researchers to study Thai sexuality for a graduate degree from a Thai university, contended that you cannot usefully define Tom or Dee as static categories, but rather positions on a continuum. She stated:

> For my thesis, I found out that there are many kinds of Tom and many kinds of Dee. Extreme Tom and Dees try to imitate their lifestyle like a heterosexual couple. They don't have the chance to see that they can have another style of relationship. Because they are socialized in a heterosexual family, they take this kind of a relationship. They have a couple in the same gender. (Lek, personal communication, 13 May 1996)

Lek, who had a long-term relationship with a *farang* lesbian, no longer considered herself strictly Tom or Dee. She believed other Tom and Dees would also resist strict categorical identification if they were exposed to alternatives. "If they have the chance, I believe some of them would change." *Anjaree* is one place where this chance is offered.

Founded by Anjana Suvarnananda in 1985, *Anjaree* has over five hundred Thai members, over half of whom live in Bangkok and over one hundred of which socialize at gatherings and meetings sponsored by the organization. Membership in *Anjaree*—someone who follows nonconformist ways—does not require the acknowledgment of specific identities or desires: Suvarnananda welcomes any woman who pays the nominal yearly dues. When introducing the term *yingratying* she posited: "We are not sure if this term will go down well or if this will be the term we stick to or not. We are in the process of building our own culture and terminologies" (1996). Her ease with new words and their reception reflects Suvarnanda's commitment to the language and the dynamics of the community she represents. While Suvarnananda speaks both for and about the women who belong to the organization she started and runs, she is also in dialogue with them. Whether or not they adopt the term will determine its usefulness: members participate in the decision-making processes about how they will imagine and describe themselves.

One member asserted that the increasingly varied positionings between the poles of Tom and Dee described by some women was limited to members of *Anjaree*. "*Anjaree* is an exception, where people want to be more ambiguously defined" (Meo, personal communication, 1996). She attributed this to the class and level of education achieved by the members—although there are *Anjaree* members around the country who receive *Anjaree*'s newsletters, most of the women that attend social events are middle-class, financially stable, single women living in Bangkok. A woman who attended for the first time *Anjaree*'s monthly event at the Bangkok cafe targeted for gay clientele, Utopia, enumerated what makes members of *Anjaree* different from what she normally sees:

1. The number of women present at the events. "Normally you just come across one friend in the workplace who identify as lesbian or Tom." *Anjaree* events often have over fifty women in attendance.

2. The age of the active members. "I've seen younger people such as university students dress in ways that appear to be Tom, but not middle age [20s through 40s] outside of *Anjaree*."

3. The class of women in attendance, which she termed

mostly "upper-middle-class."

4. "All of the lesbians I know who participate in Non-Government Organizations [including *Anjaree*] are activists who don't express themselves through certain styles of dress or hairstyles. *Anjaree* has opened up a space for another kind of identity that is neither Tom nor Dee. You can look like an ordinary woman or not, you can dress up or not, you can take care of your hair or leave it." (Ann, personal communication, 1996)

This woman found *Anjaree* unique in that it consisted of an educated, financially independent group of mature women supporting each other's efforts to construct many kinds of alternative identities.

In addition to noticing engagement in the way this specific group of women who belong to *Anjaree* present and describe themselves, she believed involvement with *Anjaree* encouraged her to resist prescribed positions. "My confidence about not having to identify myself with either side [Tom or Dee] comes from *Anjaree*. ... If I didn't know *Anjaree* I might have to think about how to identify myself within the relationship" (Ann, personal interview, 1996). This woman and her partner do not place themselves within the Tom/Dee dynamic, and neither of them conforms physically to definitions of Tom. The older woman, established in her career, carries most of the financial burden, and either or both women can initiate emotional and physical involvement.

Varaporn Chamsanit, a journalist and former Non-Government

Organization worker, believed that her knowledge about and contact with *Anjaree* illustrated that there were many political perspectives about women-who-love-women in circulation and that choices for presenting oneself were available. Although—as Sinnott argues (2004)—it would not be difficult for Varaporn to decide not to be a Dee based on assumptions about the fluidity of the Dee community, it is through *Anjaree* that Varaporn was comfortable with the politics of resisting a label. As a professional, Varaporn thinks it is important that she not be classified as a woman-who-loves-women. When she wrote about women loving women or *Anjaree* and when colleagues saw her socializing with Toms, some laughed about it and asked her if she was, in her words, a lesbian. Feeling uncomfortable about replying affirmatively, she would answer, "Why should I tell you?" which effectively stopped further questions. This is because she believes that if people see you as not heterosexual, that is the only aspect of you they think about; whereas if you are heterosexual, "They think about all you do, work, interests, whatever" (Chamsanit, personal communication, 1998). She attributed her ability to strategically position herself from contact with *Anjaree*.

Suvarnananda believed that her identity does not represent other Thai women in same-sex relationships. As a result of her education at Hague and her extensive contact and involvement with women from western, as well as non-western, cultures, Suvarnananda described her experiences and identification as atypically Thai. All of her serious relationships have been with *farang* women, and she did not place herself in either the Tom/Dee or the *farang* lesbian categories. The creation of the term *yingrakying* addressed her inability to use existing vocabulary. When attempting to classify herself, she sounded uncertain, stating that while she is neither Tom nor Dee, "I am more in the Dee category. I was pushed into this category because everyone wanted me to be in one or the other. I couldn't make a choice" (Suvarnananda, personal communication, 1996). Because of the many cultures she has experienced, she found herself in a new, previously unarticulated position, yet she is dedicated to the Thai community and situated herself within it even as she attempted to alter it so that it could incorporate her. Suvarnananda frequently discussed the difficulties she has imagining herself with the available vocabulary to *Anjaree* members, providing a model for other women to question their identities and position themselves based on their individual experiences.

While Suvarnananda supported members who wish to redefine their identities, she did not directly promote it. The majority of members still identified themselves as Tom or Dee, but an increasing number of middle-class women in their thirties, educated, and aware of the increasing number of choices available to them, no longer felt that they belonged in the one of these two categories. They consistently used Tom and Dee constructions, however, in their explanations of how they imagined themselves, positioning themselves somewhere in between or combining stereotypical features of both. The continued use of Tom and Dee to describe positions that do not adhere to the ways in which these categories have been constructed illustrates a dearth of words available to these women with which to define themselves. While the word lesbian may seem a viable alternative, Thai women continually resist using it when describing themselves. While most women used the terms Tom and Dee exclusively to describe Thai women loving women when speaking in English, some women would use the word lesbian when talking about a group; this might be because they did not know alternative words. Only one woman I interviewed reported that she was a lesbian, but she also described her position within the Tom and Dee dynamic.

When I asked Pari where she situated herself, she, like the other women I interviewed in *Anjaree*, resisted both categories. She explained that she dressed more like a man than a woman, and more like a Tom, but she said, "I don't perceive myself as a man," therefore she is not a Tom. Shortly after she explained, "I associate Tom with a person who wants to be a man--I am not a Tom because I don't want to be." Whether she does not want to be a man or a Tom was not clarified. She attributed some of her masculine habits to her position within her family. Her mother is divorced and there were no men in the house. So Pari took the role of a *lookchai*, or son. "My mom saw me as a person who does the things in a house like a *lookchai*—more than a man." Her style of dress and her role were never discussed explicitly and there was no pressure for her to change her style or habits, "Except when we go to weddings and Mom wants me to dress *riaproi* [appropriately]" (Pari, personal communication, 1996).

Providing an environment conducive to re-imagining one's sexual identity is only one of *Anjaree*'s projects. Suvarnananda and other members of the administration enumerated *Anjaree*'s primary goals as follows: community building; providing members with resources and information so that they do not feel abnormal, isolated, or alone; and offering support and advice to women who write letters of inquiry to the newsletter, *Anjaree Sarn*. Because a substantial number of members do not belong to the middle-class or live in Bangkok, they may not have contact with other women-who-love-women or access to information about Tom and Dee identity construction. For working-class women and those who place themselves strictly within the Tom/Dee dynamic, *Anjaree* provides opportunities to form liaisons, both written and social, by publishing a newsletter that encourages members to read, write, and respond to others' writings and organizes social events where women can meet. I consistently received letters from women I met at *Anjaree* events. Writing plays an important role in establishing friendships—the newsletter is filled with letters encouraging responses and social events always concluded with address swapping. Despite *Anjaree's* quickly augmenting membership, women frequently write that they feel they are the only woman-who-loves-women "in the world or in Thailand," according to Suvarnananda. Since this role is manifesting itself differently than in the past, Suvarnananda believed that many women have no examples or role models, and they can't ask for advice from their parents. Toms in many parts of Thailand can create bonds through *Anjaree Sarn*, writing about the problems they face, their identities, and their desires.

On 3 February 1996, *Anjaree* sponsored a day trip to a former king's residence and the beach. Several Toms from the small destination town who were not members of *Anjaree* were encouraged by a researcher and member working in their neighborhood to join the group. *En route* to joining the group, they insisted to the researcher and me that such an organization could not possibly exist. When they entered the bus and saw the large group of women, they were too shocked to speak. They refused to address the group, and only much later in the day did they participate in conversations initiated by individual women on the bus. By the end of the day, they were asking questions of the women they had met. Moving from a stance of disbelief and shock to one of involvement and inquiry illustrated that this single encounter with *Anjaree* changed these women's conceptions not only of the sheer number, but also the activities and positionings available to *yingrakying*.

One of the most popular events that *Anjaree* has held is a beauty contest to determine "the most handsome Tom" and "the most beautiful Dee. " Beauty contests are immensely popular in Thailand, occurring at local levels including small villages and schools, as well as regionally and nationally. Many women participate enthusiastically because winning provides an opportunity to increase one's social standing, earn a great deal of money in advertising or promotion, and/or meet rich men who eagerly provide for these beautiful women and their families. In his essay entitled "Sister Number One: the Television Production of Miss Thailand in State, Consumer, and Transnational Space," William Callahan traced the development of beauty contests and noted how they are increasingly marketed to women rather than men. The success of this marketing strategy translated to all women in the Thai community, including members of *Anjaree*. Thus beauty contests among the members have received special attention. *Anjaree*'s beauty contests, which award only small monetary prizes and vociferous, enthusiastic recognition, are enacted by women for women, simultaneously replicating and revising the way in which participants are objectified by their audiences. Rather than replicating a standardized definition of beauty, the *Anjaree* beauty contests provided chances to perform the positions of Tom and Dee in front of a sympathetic audience. The assessment by participants and members of a friendly community encouraged community building and provided all of those present with models to emulate, revise, and/or refute.[50] The construction of gender was rendered visible in these productions, enabling participants and viewers to reimagine their own position in the Tom/Dee scenario.

Political Terms

In addition to organizing and leading social events, setting up meetings and delegating tasks, coordinating the publication of the newsletter, publicizing *Anjaree* and keeping track of the increasing number of members, Suvarnananda has expended significant time and effort linking Thai women to international lesbian communities. She has established links with international organizations that work to promote community building and communication at the international level as well as supporting efforts by and speaking on behalf of institutions that link lesbian rights with human rights. She has organized two Bangkok-based international forums (1990 and 1997) that focused on women-who-love-women in Asia. In addition, Suvarnananda has provided over

---

50 This is similar to the retelling of traditional Thai folktales that takes place each night at DJ Station. See Chapter Two.

one hundred interviews to Thai and international journalists, researchers, and academics both inside and outside of Thailand, patiently answering any questions, even those that are hostile or homophobic. The press has occasionally focused on Suvarnananda's political protests, in some instances reducing *Anjaree* to a "lesbian rights group." The following appeared in *The Nation* on 12 February 1996:

> A Thai lesbian rights group has sent a protest letter to the Savings Cooperatives of Thailand (SCT) for advertising two job vacancies with a proviso that applicants must neither behave like or be homosexuals. ... The group, which calls itself *Anjaree*, described the SCT advertisement as discriminatory and in violation of basic human rights, because being a homosexual or having a criminal record have no bearing on what the job entails.

The article depicted *Anjaree* as political, actively protesting discriminatory practices. Many members would be surprised by Suvarnananda's actions in the name of *Anjaree*; like non-members, they adhere to the dominant belief that outspoken interventions are inappropriate. The majority of members in *Anjaree*, as the majority of Thai society, eschew political interventions premised on sexuality or sexual actions. *Anjaree* is perceived by them to be a social group, not a political one. Suvarnananda has used the name of her organization in her political work because institutional protests are potentially more powerful than those of a relatively unknown individual. Yet in her activism, Suvarnananda has protested on behalf of a collective without the consent of its members.

One reason that Suvarnananda has consistently supplied the sole description of Thai women loving women is her ability to speak English and provide explanations using English-language conventions. In much of mainstream Thai society, tolerance exists for actions and sexualities as long as they are not verbally announced. Thus Toms can exist, in noticeable numbers in Bangkok, and enjoy increasing popularity. In recent years, Toms have fan clubs among their female friends, and there are occasional magazines featuring Toms who are pop stars, singers, or athletes. But sex and sexuality is glaringly absent despite this visibility. The practice of verbally coming out is considered unnecessary, undesirable, and specifically western by Thai women who know of the process. Rosalind Morris has written of the difficulty women-who-love-women face when discussing sexuality:

> For the women [who love women in Thailand], sexual agency in the public domain is already transgressive, and the refusal of a reproductive domesticity is potentially antinational…not concerned with sex so much as the ways in which their relationships will be perceived by family and community members. The decision to enact public intimacy had frequently been described to me as the most demanding, the most painful, and the most politically dangerous undertaking a person can conceive. (Morris, 1997, p. 70)

Morris's description highlighted the many things at stake for women who speak about sexual desire. Respectful behavior in Thailand includes not telling the truth rather than saying something that would offend the listener or disrupt societal expectations. But in addition to seeming offensive, this kind of expression may be considered "antinational" and isolating. Consequently, many women do not want to speak out about their nontraditional identities or non-mainstream actions and express dislike or discomfort of outspoken political interventions such as protestations against homophobia or human rights assertions. While they may present themselves in a manner that publicly identifies them as women-who-love-women (particularly in the case of Toms), most women stop short of verbally announcing their identification or desires. This silence can occur even when positions seem obvious: two Toms may have a close friendship and spend a great deal of time with each other, yet never speak about their positions as Toms with each other (even when, as I described above, they try to pinpoint other Toms). Participation in *Anjaree* often includes writing about desires, and membership entails a tacit acknowledgement that one identifies with a community based on women loving women, but this never needs to be spoken.

Increasingly, however, English-language representations enact outspoken examples that counter Thai conventions. Images of sex and sexuality, as well as enunciations of desire or identity, originate from Hollywood, western advertising firms, or other non-Thai sources. As I have previously outlined, global communications have provided access to the English language, and as a result, western ideas. Both imported and Thai-produced goods and services reflect interests in trends and practices that occur outside of Thailand's borders. Consequently, English has provided a medium where Thai practices of silence about sexuality and desire can be broken. Many of the women I interviewed found it much easier to discuss their identifications and desires in English than in Thai, and many of my Thai friends preferred confessing desire to me than to their other Thai friends.[51] Suvarnananda has positioned herself and her organization according to English-language conventions when she has described sexual actions or decried homophobic practices.

Hundreds of Toms and Dees exist in Bangkok outside of *Anjaree*. Many do not know of the organization; some are reluctant to get involved. At least ten middle-class women living in Bangkok with whom I discussed *Anjaree* showed no interest; women whom I regularly socialized with refused to attend an event sponsored by *Anjaree*. These women provided a variety of reasons for their reluctance—no time, enough friends and/or social events, no interest in meeting strangers with unknown backgrounds, no interest in community building, fear of meeting the members, fear of being discovered participating in such an outspoken organization clearly premised on sexuality. Aligning oneself with an organization based on sexuality violates Thai norms requiring silence about sexual practices, so women who perceived it as sexuality-based considered *Anjaree* taboo. These women, like Pui whom I quoted portraying herself as an inferior imitation of a man, are more likely to position themselves squarely within the established categories. In contrast to this, women who have had more exposure to western imagery and ideas as well as those proficient in English often engage in the process of changing identifications in order to relate their specific situations. While

---

51 Other researchers in Thailand such as Susan and Carol concurred that their Thai informants and friends expressed similar ease in expressing these issues in English. Sinnott discusses this in *Toms and Dees* (2004).

this engagement is in dialogue with exposure to non-Thai ideas and the English language, it does not duplicate these sources. Instead, these experiences offer a means to redefinition that does not directly violate Thai values put forth and embedded in the Thai language. English may provide distance and vocabulary necessary for reevaluation, not simply models for replication. Suvarnananda insists that she has reevaluated her position as a result of being involved with *farang*, living and traveling in western countries, doing extensive research about western feminist theories, and establishing international dialogues; she has not become a lesbian per se, but has realigned herself based on her experiences and has encouraged other *yingrakying* to do the same.

I do not mean to assert that all Thai-*farang* interactions lead to changes in the way one imagines oneself; conflicts and confusions may reduce one's possibilities for self-depiction. Lek enumerated the extensive difficulties she encountered during her relationship with a *farang* woman, "Different language; different way to interpret; culture and many factors." She stated that her *farang faen* "didn't understand my kiss." In addition, "It takes many energies to explain things to a different culture." Her relationship also confounded her friends and family. "[m]y friends asked why I want a *farang faen*? Thai people still have communication problems—how can people from two different cultures get along?" (Lek, personal communication, 1996) She felt that her *faen* was very different from her and did things that were sometimes unacceptable to Thais. For example, when they moved into a new apartment, there was a video/radio shop nearby. This shop would play their movies and music so loud that it disturbed them in their apartment down the street. Her *faen* went to the shop and demanded that they reduce the volume. This assumption that one individual's comfort was worth disrupting what appeared to be compatible with society as well as the boldness she displayed by scolding a stranger was inconceivable according to Thai values. Despite Lek's shock and disapproval of her *faen*'s actions, she did internalize certain aspects of it. Our interview took place in a restaurant where the music grew progressively louder. At one point, Lek asked the waitress to turn down the music. As Lek had already explained, this presumption of individual rights is surprising and unconventional by Thai social standards. Yet she did not comment on her actions, nor did she act as if she had just done something out of the ordinary. Lek thus imagines herself in the same way as before her relationship despite what seemed to me to be evidence to the contrary.

The emergence of women who speak about and reimagine *yingrakying* has opened up new avenues in which to think Thai women-who-love-women articulating their multiple desires and identifications. Involvement in *Anjaree* has enabled this by providing social events, opportunities for oral and written communication, and community formation. Suvarnananda and her organization have responded to current situations in Thailand, helping members translate *farang* and other concepts and encouraging nomenclature such as Tom and Dee to remain flexible in meaning about those whom they denote.

The Ink's not Just Pink

Before *Anjaree San,* there was nothing published in English *by* Thai women-who-love-women about their identity constructions or positionings. There were several magazines, such as *Thai Guys,* that were English language monthlies geared for gay western tourists. They offered tourist recommendations, pictures of local Thai men, and some brief translations of Thai male erotica or short current events pieces.[52] In November 1997, *Pink Ink: Thailand's Gay and Lesbian Monthly,* began monthly publication. Printed by Utopia, the bar and publishing house Utopia where *Anjaree* often held its monthly social gatherings. *Pink Ink,*became first English-language magazine in Thailand specifically targeting a gay and lesbian local and Thai readership. Jennifer Bliss, author and co-editor, co-wrote several features with Crab Boy, a self described Tom, concerning Thai lesbians and Thai Toms, and collaborated, to provide monthly perspectives about Toms and issues concerning women-who-love-women in Bangkok. Bliss' pen name, both *farang* and sexualized, signals the kind of outspoken discussions she has provided as a *kathoey* and English speaker. The monthly commentaries with Crab Boy centered on Crab Boy's perspective as Thai and Tom, Thai and lesbian, and social, political, and cultural issues of political and family issues. Their co-authored titles such as "Lesbofile," "Butch Among the Straights," and "Braving Worlds of Disapproval" discuss how

---

52 *Thai Guys* reprinted some of the translations printed in the three volumes of *The Dove Coos.* Thailand does not recognized copyright infringement so often reprints are circulated. The magazine folded, ultimately, when an online version drew attention from the Thai government and the owners were accused of circulated child pornography, a very serious crime in Thailand.

Toms positioned themselves in both mainstream and women-centered Thai communities. Bliss and Crab Boy have written articles of concern to Thai women loving women such as January 1998's headline, "Major Boost for Lesbian Rights." In December 1997, *Pink Ink* went online, joining Utopia's "Women's Resources" page, which until then was the only site on the internet that discussed Thai women loving women, a sharp contrast to the many sites online that were set up by or deal with self-identified gay Thai men. Jennifer Bliss and Crab Boy have provided important additional English-language voices to the dearth of spokespeople on the subject before 2000. Crab Boy's youth and active participation in a women-centered scene outside of *Anjaree* provided perspectives on Thai identity construction that at times reinforced but in other instances refuted statements made by Suvarnananda.

Bliss and Crab Boy's English-language articles are much less ambiguous about positions, desires, and conflicts than the information presented in verbal interviews. Once again, a *farang* practice experienced a cultural translation. Many outspoken and explicit descriptions of women loving women exist in English in the form of books, magazines, and the Internet. Access to this information provided Bliss and Crab Boy with new vocabularies to incorporate into their Bangkok oriented discussions. They used written English, both formal and colloquial, to provide information for readers and to articulate what Crab Boy faced as a Tom, creating, in effect, new ways and languages and to initiate thought and discussion in a manner similar to Suvarnananda's attempt to coin a new word.

Pink Ink's audience includes gay Thai men, *kathoey*, *yingratying*—with or without this label--and *farang* in Thailand. Crab Boy and Bliss's commentaries consistently target readers with good English comprehension, comfortable financial positions, the capacity for international travel, and awareness of global media. Quips such as "BYO mobile phone," that employ an informal American abbreviation for invitations—Bring Your Own (Bliss, "Lesbofile," 1998)—pepper her prose, assuming a knowledge of American slang and the middle-class financial status possessed by mobile phone owners. The monthly commentaries advertised international women's travel clubs, reviewed American movies such as "Chasing Amy," ("Lesbofile," 1998) and provided U.S.-specific cultural gossip, such as discussions about possible childrearing by Anne Heche and Ellen DeGeneres ("Braving Worlds of Disapproval," 1998). Sometimes they directed her comments directly to western readers, "The question asked by most foreign lesbians arriving in Bangkok is..." ("Braving Worlds of Disapproval," 1998). This targets Thai readers fluent in English and suggests they come into contact not only with *farang* but with foreign lesbians. At other times they inform their Thai readership about relevant news in Thailand or around the world. Sometimes they targeted women who want to meet Toms, regardless of nationality or race: "If you want to meet a 'high class tom boy,' the place to go is..." ("Lesbofile," 1998). Like Suvarnananda, they write to a wide variety of audiences, but while Suvarnananda carefully changed her terminology and tone to reflect each audience, *Pink Ink* consistently writes to all, using an irreverent, playful tone. The delimiting factor for the readership is that they must be educated enough to read

English. Crab Boy's contributions also take for granted that readers, Thai or tourists, are middle/upper class as they have expendible income to frequent Bangkok bars, cafés, and clubs. Thus class, not country of origin or ideology, becomes the difference in the mode of communication between Suvarnanda and *Pink Ink*.

Pink Ink has advertised *Anjaree* events and illustrated the advances made by the existence of *Anjaree* and the work of Suvarnananda. They see *Anjaree* and Utopia as the main venues in which Crab Boy has encountered friendship and community building. Crab Boy explained in "Butch Among the Straights," "Before I discovered *Anjaree* and Utopia, I was alone among straights and had only two or three gay friends" (Bliss and Crab Boy, 1997, p. 6). Featuring Suvarnananda's conference on lesbian rights in one article, "Major Boost for Lesbian Rights," Bliss and Crab Boy not only reported the event, but provided a personal interview with Suvarnananda to further explicate the political importance of Suvarnananda's ideas and the impact of *Anjaree*. "In an interview with *Pink Ink*...Anjana [Suvarnananda]added that some people use the myth of homosexuality as mental illness to violate our rights" (Bliss and Crab Boy, 1998). They ended this article in their characteristic playful tone by quoting Suvarnananda at her most challenging: "We would like to see more discussion, particularly in academic circles, of the other aspects of the debate apart from the mental disorder issue. It's time to move beyond the kindergarten level" (Bliss, 1998).

Pink Ink's refusal to be politically correct could be considered antifeminist by Suvarnananda or the feminist English-language journalists of *The Nation* and *The Bangkok Post*. Crab Boy and Bliss dubbed Crab Boy's fellow *Anjaree* members "those lovely *Anjaree* gals" (Bliss, "Lesbofile," 1998) and encouraged the objectification of women, although reversing the still dominant *farang* practice of exotizing Asian bodies. "Lesbofile," reads: "Did you see the recent issue of the Thai-language magazine Elle with the four naked *farang* women on the cover? Way to go, Elle!" (Bliss, 1998). Yet in their discussions about why many Thai women "hide their sexuality," they used words stronger than those of Suvarnananda, accusing women of "self-hatred" (Bliss, "Braving Worlds," 1997, p. 8). Crab Boy and Bliss have tackled serious issues, and, while possibly seeming flippant in her language, has shown the same commitment and serious consideration present in Suvarnananda's work.

As I have previously outlined, Suvarnananda concerned herself primarily with three groups of women: the educated, financially secure thirty-something members of *Anjaree* who are reevaluating their positions as Toms and Dees, working-class members who write to *Anjaree Sarn* and participate in social functions, and international lesbian and feminist action groups. While *Pink Ink* also targeted this first group of women; in addition, in the columns featuring Crab Boy, it spoke to other financially secure women, both Thai and foreign, both members of *Anjaree* and those not affiliated with organizations. This Bangkok centered independent voice circulated among the social communities, encouraging a more loosely based form of networking and community with porous boundaries. While these women often had more strict definitions of their identities, *Pink Ink* has provided information about how to meet other women-who-love-women in Thailand, offered a dialogue about how Toms have constructed themselves, and contributed visions and descriptions of women loving women.

Suvarnananda was once the only spokesperson for Thai women-who-love-women. Fast forward ten years later. Now many spokespeople and publications exist, including a Thai language publication dedicated to Toms. By 2014, Toms were publically recognized, a visible presence in Bangkok and in Thailand's media. Since 2008, *Tom Act Magazine*, a predominantly Thai-language publication that can be found in magazine stands around Bangkok, has a popular annual Mr. Tom contest. This annual event continues to attract a large Thai audience and contestants appear on many popular Thailand television shows such as "Thailand's Got Talent" aired June 30, 2013.[53]

The increasing number of outlets, such as writing in English or opportunities to write for the press and the internet, has encouraged women to participate in conversations about how they imagine themselves and construct their identities. The proliferation of new interactions with the terms and accompanying stereotypes of Tom and Dee, or the realignment within these categories as practiced by members of *Anjaree*, has encouraged women-who-love-women to carve out previously unavailable identifications and identities that are in dialogue with their contemporary situations. English is no longer the preferred language for discussing Thai women's identities. Avenues wherein Thai

---

53 The Thailand's Got Talent segment featuring the Mr. Tom 2013 contestants aired June 30, 2014 can be seen on Youtube at: https://www.youtube.com/watch?v=2SQ0iieAqQU.

women articulate and situate themselves according to their contemporary circumstances emerge continually. They have provided particularly Thai configurations--not derived solely from nor imitating women outside of Thailand, yet aware of and in conversation with non-local events and media.

4

"The Weaving New Life Project": Thai Women by Thai NGOs

Images of Thai women as farmers, weavers, and mothers in the unspoiled Thai countryside or as construction workers who happily and skillfully employ modern machinery in the construction of urban Bangkok are ubiquitous on the covers of guidebooks and tourist magazines about Thailand. The Thai government and its tourism arm, the Tourism Authority of Thailand (TAT) also use them as advertisements to promote tourism. However, it's not only the promoters of tourism that use romanticized images of Thai women and project them to an international audience. In fact, English-language publications produced by women-centered Non-Government Organizations (NGOs) and the Thai government-sponsored National Commission On Women's

Affairs frequently feature images of women as idealized rural and urban producers, weavers in particular, both in textual and visual presentations, in order to attract international attention. For example, depictions of women weaving appeared in each of the following English-language publications: the *FOW Newsletter*, produced by the Friends of Women Foundation; *Voices of Thai Women*, produced by the Foundation for Women; the *GWG Newsletter*, produced by the Gender and Development Research Institute; and the government-sponsored *Women of Thailand* newsletter. Why would these Thai political organizations that work for women's equality with differing strategies all proffer ahistorical, stereotypical images of Thai women in their publications rather than focusing on visual markers of the organizations goals and achievements?

The persistent representation of women as weavers by these various Thai NGOs and government organizations illustrates a shared belief about the power of Thai women and weaving. Weaving has traditionally been thought of as women's work in most western and many non-western cultures. In "The Future Looms: Weaving Women and Cybernetics," Cultural Studies and Feminist author Sadie Plant has noted Freud's attribution of a gendered meaning to the process. "For Freud, weaving imitates the concealment of the womb: the Greek *hystera*; the Latin *matrix*. Weaving is woman's compensation for the absence of the penis, the woman of whom, as he famously insists, there is 'nothing to be seen'" (Plant, 1996, p. 123). Plant used Freud's account of masking nothing to create a metaphor yoking computer development and weaving, which extends back to the nineteenth-century. In her revised version of the development of cybernetics, Plant wrote in bold letters, **"Ada Lovelace First Weaves Women and Cybernetics Together in the 1840s"** (1996, p. 123). She continued:

> The computer emerges out of the history of weaving, a process often said to be the quintessence of women's work. The loom is the vanguard site of software development, and if Ada Lovelace makes an early encounter between woman and computer, the association between women and software throws back into the mythical origins of history. Yet the development of the computer might itself be described in terms of the introduction of increasing speed, miniaturization, and complexity to the process of weaving, which threads its way to convergence in the global data webs and communication nets of the late twentieth century. (Plant, 1996, p. 123)

By associating computer development with the practice of weaving, Plant "feminized" computer technologies. Similarly, the metaphor she developed between processes of weaving and "convergence in global data webs and communication nets" provided an image wherein the processes of globalization, especially in terms of communication, are seen as extensions of weaving. I find Plant's metaphor relevant for two reasons. First, it demonstrates the way in which weaving functions as a powerful gendered image: imagining this feminized practice as the precursor to masculine-affiliated technology development is startling and disruptive. Second, the effect of this metaphor, extending credit to women for developing processes of globalization, sets the stage for this chapter, which outlines the ways in which Thai women produce texts that respond to the changing international climate, contributing to the construction of new forms of political, economic, and social participation in a global arena where women's voices were previously excluded. The Thai women-centered NGOs and the government organization that I discuss in this chapter produced and circulated English-language representations in order to shape perceptions of and by underrepresented Thai women. Consequently, in order to reach their goals, these organizations targeted international, English-speaking audiences, and in a manner similar to Plant's software genealogy, they employed traditionally gendered images such as weaving and link them to global concerns such as guaranteeing human rights.

This chapter will examine the types of representations that are circulated by Bangkok-based women-centered NGOs and the government-sponsored National Commission On Women's Affairs for non-Thai consumption. I examine English-language documents in order to ascertain the strategies for representation for a complicated audience that exceeds Thai citizens located within the borders of the nation. First, I show how NGOs have enabled amplified international acceptance of the existence of fundamental human rights. Implying that international organizations have a responsibility to work toward the achievement of woman's/human rights, Thai NGOs strategically call for support to achieve their agendas. To situate these practices, I outline the development and position of Thai women-centered NGOs vis-á-vis the

Thai government. I then analyze the use of images of women weaving in three English-language articles by the Friends of Women Foundation (FOW) and the Foundation for Women (FFW). Next, I consider the competing practices of representation related to me by Dr. Saisuree Chutikul of the National Commission On Women's Affairs and Dr. Suteera Thomson of the Gender and Development Research Institute (GDRI). Finally, I delineate the practices of the NGO, EMPOWER, which, contrary to these other women-centered NGOs, promoted the self-representation by Bangkok-based Thai sex-workers for a local rather than international foreign audience. This catalog of innovative initiatives by these groups illustrates that these women are not only responding to the changing conditions brought about by globalization, they are also shaping the way in which gender, Thai, and third-world women, and human rights are understood.

The 1990s, following the highly attended, highly publicized NGO Forums on Women and the UN Third and Fourth World Conferences on Women (in Nairobi and Beijing, respectively), have seen renewed prominence of the discourse of human rights in international relations. By foregrounding women's rights in the language of human rights and using the language celebrated by the UN, the newsletters mentioned above linked Thai women to those of all women, all people, and made their causes inalienable through the discourse of universality and human rights. However, the concerns of these NGOs are not necessarily identical to those of women in other countries. Consequently, the images deployed by these Thai, women-centered NGOs differ in some respects from strategies for representing women created by NGOs based in other countries. While feminists from "developed" (ie. Western) countries are constantly touting global sisterhood as essential for future "progress" many NGOs from the global south have noted the dangers involved in following identical strategies to those developed by western feminism. These forums provided the impetus for using the universal human rights language to inform the arguments for women's equality. Accordingly, Thai NGOs deployed human rights discourses in order to promote their specific women-centered agendas to a transnational audience. Indeed, Thai NGOs looked outward using UN sponsored human rights language, carefully shaping their positions and forging unusual alignments.[54]

The work done by these NGOs contrasts sharply with previous non-government interventions that were premised on the belief that nations follow a trajectory: non/under-developed, developing, developed. Development justifies and contributes to the spread of western culture by privileging the capitalist model. In *Global Dreams*, Richard Barnet and John Cavanagh compared this development model with that of religious conversion, "Economic development has become a leading twentieth-century secular religion, although its roots are in the eighteenth-century. ... Nations, like flowers, unfold by using their resources in prescribed ways, in short, by proceeding along a well-trodden path to something called 'development'" (Barnet, 1994, p. 287).

---

54 For example, although Asian governments and NGOs agreed on the validity of human rights, for the UN World Conference on Human Rights Asian NGOs produced their own declaration of intent that differed from that of Asian governments. See Koshy, 1999, pp. 10-18, especially page 12.

While some development plans take into account specific economic, political, or cultural conditions, the desired outcome for each nation is identical—the creation of market-oriented economies that make their resources available to foreign capital. NGOs, however, are attempting many approaches for a variety of reasons. The increasing recognition they receive from national and international political bodies allows for the creation of alternatives to standard development procedures, employing, resisting, or realigning designs currently underway.

Whether or not development—a western generated concept that often aims to replicate the industrialization processes and international market participation of the United States and certain European countries globally—remains a desirable goal for Thailand is rarely considered. While some non-western NGOs have corresponding projects, each organization created its own plan for action, recognizing that despite similarities, every country possesses unique cultural, social, and economic conditions. In *Real and Imagined Women,* globally distingued Professor of English Rajeswari Sunder Rajan described some of the shared characteristics of the ways in which countries are depicted as developing and their accompanied gender assumptions:, "'Developing' countries are also characterized by severe inequities in class, caste, community, and gender relations which generate the endemic violence characteristic of their social structures" (1993, p. 6). By terming these countries "developing," Rajan underscored the economic strategies shared by many of these governments. Focusing their study on Thailand, Tantiwiramanond and Pandey took for granted that Thailand would participate in development—the government had produced a Declaration on the Right to Development—but questioned the assessments and goals of development strategies, "Should the development process give priority to welfare or to growth, to income generation or to consciousness raising, to Western-influenced urban development or to reconstruction based on indigenous cultural roots?" (Tantiwiramanond, 1991, p. 113). They have noted that, historically, many development plans have led to increased gender inequities.

During the 1990s, there was an increase in the number of academic publications that focused on the influence exercised by NGOs on non-western governments.[55] They analyzed the potential for these organizations to highlight injustices and effect change on behalf of traditionally under-represented subjects. Some of these studies remarked on the international communication that takes place among NGOs with identical projects, but they did not examine extra-national liaisons wherein NGOs received support from non-related, non-local sources. While political theorists such as Gearoid Tuathail and Simon Dalby have argued that the "dimensionality and practices of geopolitics are being transformed by globalization and informationalization" (1998, p. 8), these studies of NGOs did not extend their considerations to reflect the interactions beyond the boundaries of the nation-state that took place.[56]

55 For example, *Nongovernments: NGOs and the Political Development of the Third World* by Julie Fisher (1998); *NGOs, The UN, and Global Governance* edited by Thomas Weiss and Leon Gordenker (1996); and "Non-Government Organizations, the State and Democratization in Indonesia" (1997) and *Non-Government Organizations and Democratic Participation in Indonesia* (1995) both by Philip J. Eldridge.

56 For extended considerations about the changing effects of travel and extending notions of cosmopolitanism, see Pheng Cheah and Bruce Robbin's collection, *Cosmopolitics: Thinking and Feeling beyond the Nation* (1998). Arjun Appadurai (1990 and 1997), whom I discussed in Chapter One, also theorizes the

While studying the transformation Tuathail and Dalby described; I also examine the materials produced by these NGOs both specifically, in dialogue with each other, as well as within a larger, transnational context.

I argue that certain Thai women-centered NGOs and the National Commission On Women's Affairs generated English representations of Thai women in response to the transnational political climate. Although the methods for portraying women varied between the organizations that I discuss, these groups consistently employed these images in English to garner international support and attention. This procedure responded to the erosion of the nation-state, contributing to the development of alternatives for imagining oneself in the world. They weaved their concerns with those of other nations and reached beyond the borders of Thailand or to foreigners visiting Thailand to solicit involvement and a shared sense of purpose. In response to pressure from the United Nations, the Thai government agreed to work toward women's equality, In order to hold the government accountable for reforming inequities according to international agreements, external agencies both inside and outside of Thailand were allowed to advise and facilitate this change. I will thus explore the ways in which these links are solicited, isolating what can loosely be termed as three groups of strategies, and examining the conflicts and questions involved therein.

Situating Thai NGOs

The emergence of women-centered NGOs in Thailand began

---

extension of national belonging.

with the student movement of the early 1970s that—initially based on the new left Marxism promoted by students in the west—critiqued a wide range of Thai social, political, and economic practices. Demonstrations and discussions moved from protesting what the leading political and economic historians of Thailand, Pasuk Phongpaichit and Chris Baker, have "*symptoms*—bureaucratic malpractice, labour problems, educational administration, and high prices" to considering how to dismantle the "*causes*—the US presence, the role of the military, and the power of capitalism" (Phongpaichit and Baker, 1996, p. 305).[57] While women-centered issues were not explicitly addressed, these reevaluations of Thailand's circumstances paved the way for evaluations of gender inequities. Furthermore, since these protests coincided with economic growth and the emergence of a stable Thai middle-class, material support for new agendas for reform made the establishment of NGOs possible during the 1970s.[58] In her study of Thai NGOs, Amara Pongsapich found that "Most public-spirited developmental non-profit organizations established during this period…are middle class organizations, in contrast to the ones developed earlier which were set up mainly of members from the upper class" (1995, p. 38). The increase in

---

57 These authors provide the most complete account of Thai history and politics. Pages 304-14 describe the student movement (1996).

58 Nerida Cook describes this class as follows: "Class is a necessarily relational phenomonenon, and the usage here is intended to highlight the way in which many of these women contrast themselves both with the rural majority, and with a wealthy sector of urban society associated with traditional forms of power and with a conservative world view" (1998, p. 251). She suggests that the goals and strategies of Thai activists (especially in terms of their approach to prostitutes) "is constituted by the class-based nature both of their own 'modern' subjectivities, and of the gendered explanatory frameworks they have utilised" (1998, p. 251).

the number of organizations meant an expansion in the types of projects and procedures for their implementation.

The ideologies of these NGOs differed from previous women's groups operating as social clubs or philanthropies, consisting largely of elite, upper-class women. Anthropologist Nerida Cook explained that these new NGOs "explor[ed] the applicability of Western feminism—to which they have increased access" and "develop[ed] their own views of the limitations of the older elite women's groups" (Cook, 1998, p. 257). Two aspects of feminist activism seemed most applicable; Tantiwiramanond and Pandey have asserted that almost all Thai women's NGOs "absorbed the Western concepts of starting women's 'projects' and of 'enhancing the status of women'" (1991, p. 145). Other goals of western feminism, such as changing relations between men and women, have not been addressed by Thai NGOs. With the establishment of new women-centered NGOs in the 1980s and 90s, constituencies and approaches began to differ (Tantiwiramanond, 1991, p. 145). Cook attributed this to changing historical circumstances, "Thai women's organisations fairly consistently reflect the respective values of the particular classes, times and political conditions of their origins. This leads to varied responses to central issues of concern to newer women's groups..." (1998, p. 260). Older groups persisted and new ones, responding to changing issues, developed. The class-based origins from their inception and accompanying assumptions about how best to represent Thai women and Thai culture account for much of why the strategies for representation among these groups varied.

Although the NGOs have different projects, they frequently

came together. Phongpaichit explained, "When important issues concerning women are recognized, these groups join hands and establish quite a strong network working for causes of concern to all women" (personal interview, 1996). Their overall effect within the government, however, is sometimes seen to be lacking. For example, in *The World of Thai Women*, Chitra Ghosh generalized about the changing position of Asian and Thai women, describing westernization rather than equality as the most evident form of progress. "But as in every other Asian country Thailand is steeped in the ancient value system, though progress has been remarkable in dress, fashion and other aspects of one's life—in imitating the western mode and pattern" (Ghosh, 1990, p. 222). Ghosh understood NGOs as working toward improving the situation of women, yet found their position marginal when compared with the power held by the conservative government and Buddhist authorities. She wrote, "Many Non-Government Organizations have become quite vociferous and active. But the real authority and the ultimate decision making power has not yet evolved on the large number of ordinary women who make up the majority of the female population of Thailand" (Ghosh, 1990, p. 223). Since members of the Thai government often argued that "rights" are neither Thai nor Asian concepts (Pongsapich, personal interview, 1996), rights may be ignored or championed, depending on the circumstances, government agencies or Thai officials. However, the position of Thai women-centered NGOs as outside "the real authority and the ultimate decision making power" may have led them to seek support beyond the national government. In their attempt to establish certain rights to Thai women, they asserted that these rights exist on a global level, internationalizing what was formerly considered a contract between individual nation-states and their citizens.

The international attention garnered from employing human rights discourses in English, in addition to the increasing recognition of Thai NGOs by the Thai government, has been fueled by the increasing recognition overall of NGOs by the United Nations[59] and NGOs mounting insistence on the universality and indivisibility of human rights (Robbins, 1999, p. 140). Since Thailand's Fourth National Development Plan (1977-1981) that marked the first government women in development program,[60] the argument that women's rights fall under the rubric of human rights has been successfully employed by Thai NGOs. This permits domestic injustices against Thai women to be considered international human rights violations, encouraging external censure. It also invites external funding for domestic projects.

Receiving external funding and attracting international awareness has enabled many NGOs to negotiate a position where they can push for government action while resisting government control. Amara Pongsapich believed that Thai NGOs engaged the Thai government at key junctures "to influence government policies on issues related to women" (Pongsapich, 1996). Thus NGOs and government in Thailand enmeshed and interacted—they were not seen as opposing bodies. The

---

59 Robbins pp. 139-44. Robbins charts "the dramatically increased impact, especially since the end of the cold war, of the so-called NGOs. . ." (1999, p. 139).

60 Including policies about women and youth was, according to Amara Pongsapich ("*Feminism Theories*", 1996), a response to the United Nations declaration that 1975 was to be International Women's Year and 1976-85 the Decade of Women.

clear missions and international support of Thai women-centered NGOs afforded them independence and influence unique to this particular historical juncture. Rajan has theorized this type of NGO intervention in non-Thai settings, where NGOs are able to both influence the government and resist its control: "The women's movement ends by both forming alliances with the state—typically in the form of seeking the recourse of its laws in instituting legal reform or enacting new laws on behalf of women—as well as resisting the state's control, which is precisely a consequence of the powers vested in it" (Rajan, 1993, p. 6). Linking human rights to women's rights and establishing external accountability allows NGOs to achieve this delicate balance.

The increasing acceptance by national governments of the tenets outlined in the Declaration of Human Rights and, by extension, the validation of women's rights, have altered the way in which third-world women imagine themselves and are imagined, extending the responsibility for rectifying inequities beyond the borders of the nation-states in which they occur. NGOs were strategically positioned in a public sphere between the state and the non-state, intersecting with both local and global frameworks. In thinking about globalization and cosmopolitan localities, cultural theorist Bruce Robbins argued that a universalizing of human rights discourses has emerged, and human rights now function "as an instrument whose power cannot be wholly or permanently circumscribed."[61] The efforts made by NGOs to affect government practices on behalf of human rights has altered previous

---

61 1999, p. 74. See pp. 72-77 for a more lengthy consideration of the universalization of human rights discourses with examples of international interventions made on their behalf.

boundaries for involvement and intervention by non-government agencies, affecting a new global public sphere in which individual nation-states are held accountable for the treatment of their citizens by extra-national organizations.

The evocation of human rights doctrines by Thai NGOs to attract international support, applying technologies developed outside of Thailand to proliferate their messages, is similar to other procedures Thais have followed to safeguard their interests. As I have previously noted, apropos of gendered language, Thailand has a history of adapting *farang* words for their own use. But often customs and ideas are not only adapted; many instances exemplify the ability to master *farang* customs and ideas when necessary. This understanding was displayed by King Mongkut (1851-1868) who constructed the borders of Thailand in response to colonization by the British of neighboring Burma. The notion of a boundary demarcating the nation of Thailand as beginning and ending at a specific line on the earth seemed ridiculous to Thai rulers; people constituted the Thai empire. Boundaries in Thailand were considered the area that a town or empire could protect. Boundaries were not negotiable between rulers because they were porous, changing with the movement of the local population. They could not be physically demarcated in any way. Efforts by the British to establish a border dividing Thailand from Burma must have seemed unfriendly, because they resulted in confrontations. Despite these conflicts, the existence of different concepts of political space went unnoticed for some time. Yet after repeated efforts by the British to increase their territory, King

Mongkut and his contemporaries learned the western concept and adopted it, using it to their advantage and extending their territory by gaining the allegiance of local subjects. Although these conceptions were at odds with their own understanding of space and empire, Thai leaders were able to understand them, employing them to their advantage. The British, on the other hand, never acknowledged a differing perspective.[62] Emerging from these histories, Thai NGOs deployed similar abilities to understand and retool the humanist ideology underlying the application of human rights discourses.

When choosing representations of Thai women, women-centered NGOs targeted non-Thai readers. These NGOs were aware of the difficulties of representing Thai women, especially those from backgrounds dissimilar to middle-class NGO workers, and this was reflected in the choices of images that appear in their newsletters. The four women I interviewed involved in the writing and production of these newsletters each stressed that they considered, with each issue, the ramifications of creating an international, English-language newsletter. Usa Lerdsrisuntad of the Foundation for Women described in detail the difficulties the staff faced about issues of representation. Four or five of the staff had extended discussions about which topics each newsletter would cover. Usa explained that they wanted to "show strong women not like the picture people normally see about Thai women" (personal interview, 1996). As a result, most of the NGOs producing English-language representations employed a native English speaker to provide

---

62 Tongchai Winichakul provides this excellent analysis in *Siam Mapped* (1994).

contextualization for their readers. Pam Simmons, author and editor of the English-language publication *Voices of Thai Women* produced by the Foundation for Women (FFW), based her choices on what her Thai co-workers told her and what she observed happening in the organization from her non-Thai perspective. Then she gave her work to her Thai colleagues to read and correct. Simmons explained that in this publication, "It's not Thai women on their own representing themselves to a foreign audience. It's through a foreign woman" (Simmons, personal interview, 1996). While Pam acknowledged her role in representing these women, she distinguished a hierarchy of mediation. She believed that she could more accurately present the "voices of Thai women" than those outside the organization. Before Pam began working full time at the NGO, the publication consisted of an introduction by the FFW and a series of articles reprinted from the local English-language daily newspapers, *The Bangkok Post* and *The Nation*. The Foundation reproduced previously published articles that they believed provided their international audience "current information about Thai women and Thai women's interests" (Lerdsrisanthad, personal communication, 1996). According to Simmons, her involvement with the organization and the dialogues she conducted with the Thai FFW staff positioned her differently than other foreign women. She stated, "My own understanding is absolutely dependent on being here day after day after day." When other *farang* volunteers offered to write articles for the publication, Pam refused, "I don't know whether that's possible. I mean they could write them as foreign journalists but this magazine is about voices of Thai women" (Simmons, personal interview, 1996).

When producing English-language documents for international consumption, direct translations from Thai documents were not often used. Thai women-centered NGOs and the National Commission On Women's Affairs (NCWA) realized the importance of clear, accurate wording to explain their projects and engage their audience. Dr. Saisuree Chutikul, director of the NCWA, outlined the problems of translation from Thai to English, citing three obstacles to successful translation. First, she explained, "Thai language is able to put in a sentence" ideas that cannot be replicated "according to the logic of the use of English. The sentence structures are different and so the very work of doing it is very difficult" (Chutikul, personal interview, 1995). Translating paragraph-to-paragraph rather than sentence-to-sentence facilitated the adherence to English grammar and sentence structure, but this broad style of translation often resulted in the omission of information and changes in overall meaning and effect. Secondly, there was a dearth of qualified translators. Because English language fluency was not widespread, direct translations were often incomprehensible. An English-speaking editor might have be hired to make sense of translations, but a second editor would not refer to the original text. If the document was not subsequently reedited against the Thai original, misinterpretations through extensive rewording were inevitable. Finally, the cost of translation was enormous by NGO and government standards, as demand was high and foreign businesses could afford to pay internationallycompetitive salaries. Thus substandard editors who did incomplete or inaccurate work were sometimes employed.

Although these NGOs understood the premises of human rights discourses, issues of maintaining their voices and translation stood out during my interviews with the writers and directors. Thus their methods varied widely. The following sections look at specific articles within these English language publications in order to query: Can these organizations predict how images will be received across cultural and linguistic frontiers? How can they portray women in a way that simultaneously remembers women's past roles as contributing to their communities and environment while recognizing the importance for change and improvement in their current roles? Do representations generated for international consumption operate in a global public sphere that extends rights to women situated within national borders?

"The Weaving New Life Project"

Images of weaving occur frequently in both the *Voices of Thai Women* and the *FOW Newsletter*, but they rarely referenced the production of cloth. Rather, they described the actions of women in other arenas. Combining Thai women and weaving did not create a simple, uniform image, and these newsletters exploited the historical references to Thai women and the metaphorical references in English. I will isolate three articles that employ weaving in these newsletters and examine how they work:

First, *Voices of Thai Women* newsletter frequently reports about traffic in Asian women. In 1992, it summarized the proceedings of a three-day workshop on Traffic in Asian Women. The participants of this workshop demanded to minimize sexual exploitation and reform the situation of migrant workers and sex-workers involved with service men from other countries, as well as addressing problems with the current model for development. The newsletter entitled their article on this workshop "Weaving the Asian Women's Future" and the declaration produced in the workshop also bore this designation.

Second, in December 1992 the *FOW Newsletter* featured an article entitled "Weaving Dreams in the Name of Peace" by Nilubol Pornpitagpan that discussed the art exhibit "Nine Dream Weavers for Peace." The Friends of Women Foundation organized this exhibit, which included the work of seven artists and two poets, to raise money for the upcoming Fourth War Resister's International Women's Conference.

Finally, the Foundation for Women's "Weaving New Life Project" named its overall project and served as the title of one of its issues (July 1994). The cover of this issue features a young Thai woman wearing a pasan and using a spinning wheel to make thread, most likely silk. She is sitting on a cloth on the ground, bare feet tucked under and flip-flops by her side. The photograph includes several houses on stilts in the background, with others signs, such as baskets in which animals are kept, that reflect Thai villages. The contextual clues lead to the assumption that this woman is a rural Thai weaver, yet while the Foundation for Women's project involves rural women, it does not organize textile production. The featured article in this issue is an evaluation of the "Weaving New Life Project" conducted in February 1994. The objective of the "Weaving New Life Project" was "to encourage and promote initiatives of women and youth at the grass-roots level to solve their problems and to improve their livelihood" ("Weaving," 1994, p. 12). To do this, the Foundation for Women trained para-social development workers to conduct a survey about the situation of women and youth in their communities.

Each of these examples involved women doing work, but none of them were working as weavers. In fact, all of these women, conference organizers and attendees, artists, para-social development workers, and Foundation for Women researchers, participated in work that requires education, organization, and community or institutional support beyond what many rural women weavers receive. So why invoke weaving to represent these women and their work? Weaving, in Thailand and in metaphorical English, resonates beyond the act of twisting threads. In my introduction to this chapter, I discussed the use of images of weaving women by the Tourisn Authority of Thailand (TAT) to construct an ideal version of Thailand. These newsletters are similarly employing this image, especially in the case of the *Voices of Thai Women* issue with the photograph of the weaver on its cover.

The weaving of cloth contributes both economically and culturally to Thailand. Produced initially for local consumption, the patterns and styles of cloth reflect distinct regions and methods of production. Each community in most of Thailand, Laos, and the hill-tribes in the northern mountains of Thailand produced individual patterns, colors, styles, and types of cloth. Robyn Maxwell, an expert on textiles from Southeast Asia, has written of Southeast Asian fabrics, in particular, "Gender, age, marital status, clan membership, and district or village origins may be read from a particular textile or the way in which it is worn" (1992, p.

19).[63] Women in Thailand still make and wear these cloths, and some styles are so specific that the cloth can be located past the province or village to the individual weaver. Laotians living in the Northern Thailand villages around Sisatchanalai and Uttaradit are recognized not only by their language, but also by their use of dtin sin, a "decorative, separately woven piece of fabric added to the hem of a girl's skirt" (Cheesman, 1988, pp. 130-1). These local weaving practices have been coordinated in past decades. The Queen of Thailand, several NGOs, and communities themselves have organized cottage industries where women work together, organizing production and distribution and sometimes sales of their local cloths to an increasingly interested international marketplace. Hmong refugees in Thailand still create their traditional storycloths, but the stories they tell change as their history changes. Over the past decade storycloths often describe Hmong emigration from Laos, including images of soldiers, bombs, and airplanes. (See Image 4.1) The Hmong's worldwide diaspora and increasing visibility furnishes more markets for their storycloths, and they receive far more money for their work than when it was only consumed locally.[64] And although weaving practices change in response to the demands of the marketplace and the concerns of the weavers, they also remain an art form grounded by the lives lived of the people who make them.

---

63 She explains further: "Clothing is one of the oldest functions of the textiles, and the shape of a garment, its colour, design and motif indicate important and fundamental information about the wearer" (1992, p. 19).

64 For more details, see my essay "Northwest WorldPerks: Speaking about the Hmong Diaspora from the Orientalist/Western Feminist Paradigm" (1994).

Image 4.1

Through the historically grounded and gendered image of weaving, these newsletters combined the past and the present of rural Thai women in a manner that pushed for change while respecting their histories. Rather than using weaving to disrupt gendered assumptions, they foregrounded the gendered aspect of weaving. What constitutes weaving was broadened, reflecting both earlier and current practices of Thai women. The article "Weaving the Asian Women's Future" extended the notion of Thailand as the site for fabric production by tying it to the production of culturally specific material embodied by the article itself, the workshop it recalled, and the declaration that emerged from consolidated efforts. The workshop considered the trafficking of Asian women to other countries; the image of weaving the future corresponded to the increasingly transnational consumer base for the sale of Asian cloth—part of international markets, it still retained traditional, community-specific styles. The workshop and the declaration hoped that the women who were the objects of their calls for reform could also achieve this. In an analogous fashion, the article "Weaving Dreams in the Name of Peace" used the image of weaving for an exhibition that works toward peace. Calling these women artists and poets elevates the value of weaving, linking these artists to what is considered an increasingly popular art form, not just a craft produced by women out of necessity. Associating these types of actions with the work of women weavers highlights their importance to their individual communities and the results this can have worldwide. Likewise, the FFW capitalized on the weaving image by calling their project and an article that reported it entitled "The Weaving New Life Project." Here the traditional image of Thai women again pushed past its historical connotations. This project concentrated specifically on rural women and children and what is deplorable in their current lives. Each para-social development worker worked in her own community, as weavers do (and she may have been a weaver as well since the FFW could not provide full time positions for these women), for cultural and economic improvement.

Connecting these women to the traditional role of weavers displays women in a positive light rather than as victims. Vendana Shiva, a well-known Indian environmental theorist, has written about the results of coupling women with their environment:

> Most work on women and environment in the Third World has focused on women as special victims of environmental degradation. Yet the women who participate in and lead ecology movements in countries like India are not speaking merely as victims. Their voices are the voices of liberation and transformation which provide new categories of challenge that women in ecology movements are creating in the Third World. (Shiva, 1989, p. 47)

Shiva shifted the stereotype of woman as victim associated with the yoking of women to the earth in her assessment, altering the assumptions that accompanies the parallel. Women are no longer essentially earthly bodies, they instead are the innovative forces that might liberate an endangered environment. Similarly, these NGOs took a traditional connection—that of women and cloth production—and found ways to make the link contemporary and positive. The ways in which weaving is being used to produce new positions for women and their communities are analogous to the readjustments of the correlations between women and the environment that Shiva described. The weavers of these newsletters are working to improve lives, both globally, such as with the idea of world peace, and locally, by isolating problems within specific communities. Although manufacturing these images may serve to reify their association with Thai women, changing their contexts may reinforce the vocation as affirmative, artistic, and more broad referentially, rather than as a custom of poor people with few abilities and no alternatives.

In each instance, the weaving metaphor conjured hope. In the article, "Weaving Asian Women's Future," the participants of the workshop used the image of weaving, just as the newsletter took its title from this declaration, to refer to change for women currently exploited, sexually and economically, because of relocating abroad or being involved with foreigners in their home countries. The phrase "Weaving the Asian Women's Future" has a functional connotation. While there are women were victims of sexual and economic exploitation, work was being done to create, both for and with them, a different future: the metaphor holds the promise and potential futures of an intricate cloth and these women, like the twisting strands of thread, can become integrated members of their new communities. The success of this project was clear from the title, and the potential for expansion of this project and further interventions, especially through international support, was implied.

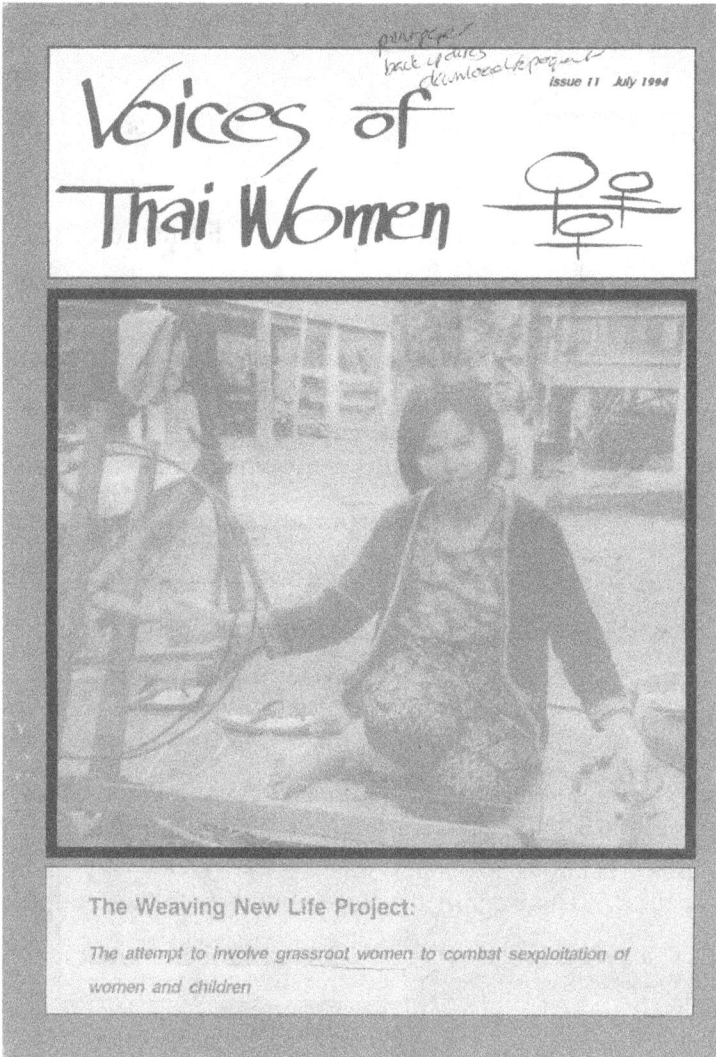

Image 4.2

In a similar fashion, using the products of women artists to raise money for a peace project called "Nine Dream Weavers for Peace" moved the representation of Thai women from the traditionally expected occupation of weaver to the influential vocation of peacemaker. None of the works mentioned in the article practices or addresses weaving, but the goal, as stated in the title, was to finance a conference against war, which, like Plant's genealogy, linked prestigious, previously male-gendered work to the practice of weaving. Thus the work of these artists not only positively represented women and their environments, it also both metaphorically and materially (the conference did take place) expanded the roles played by women in international forums.

The image of weaving also has aesthetic connotations. The woman on the cover of the *Voices of Thai Women* smiled at the camera and seemingly at the reader; her pleasant demeanor as well as her specifically Thai environment were aesthetically portrayed and, perhaps, seem exotic to a non-Thai viewer thereby encouraging further attention. Her patterned pasan reflected weaving and rural communities. Her clothing and the background details of the photograph contained rural Thai implements and architecture. All this could combine to attract readers' interest in the woman, her community, and Thailand.[65] A photograph of para-social workers, like the one that appeared within the article (19), does not have the same allure. The English language audience of these publications, for the most part donors, other NGOs and similarly interested parties, is more likely to be familiar with images of para-social workers, women in meetings or women in training courses. So by putting a less familiar, more romanticized Thai woman on the cover, the FFW hopes their publication will be noticed. When I asked the FFW why they chose the name "Weaving New Life Project" for their para-social worker training, Usa Lerdsrisuntad said it was "pretty, a nice name" (Lerdsrisanthad,

---

65 The reception of this or any other image cannot be entirely controlled. Despite the intentions of the FFW, this photograph may also inspire sexual attraction.

personal interview, 1996). The FFW realizes that it is catchy; they know people will remember it; they pay attention to aesthetics and recognize the power of a name. During the same interview, the FFW resisted calling a new project we discussed anything in English, although it already had a name in Thai, because they had not yet found a name they agreed would promote the project in light of their goals. They believe that weaving, an activity practiced worldwide, resonates outside of Thailand in a way that a more oblique reference or an exclusively Thai one would not.

However, tying the representation of women to that of weavers also has negative effects. The women being discussed in these articles hold positions still difficult for women to attain—conference organizers, artists, para-social workers, foundation coordinators, researchers, and analysts—people who actively change societies. Highlighting these occupations in the headlines and on the front cover would provide a positive image of women concretely modifying their world. Insinuating that women and weaving are intertwined perpetuates rather than shifts weaving's gendered dimensions. While these newsletters link weaving with other practices to heighten appreciation of both, it is unclear whether it does more to extend the romanticized image of Thai women or to encourage greater understanding of their conditions.

THAI WOMEN

Image 4.3

Greeting Card Photos: "Women and Work"

This section compares the strategies for representation of Thai women by two agencies that interact frequently with the Thai government. Dr. Saisuree Chutikul of the National Commission On Women's Affairs, a recently established branch of the government, and Dr. Suteera Thomson of the Gender and Development Research Institute (GDRI), a prominent NGO, each provided me with lengthy interviews assessing the strategies employed by their organizations. After Thailand's participation in the Nairobi Third World Conference on Women, in 1985 the Thai Government approved the creation of the National Commission On Women's Affairs. With funding and advice in the form of a grant from the Canadian government, it became a subsidiary of the Office of the Prime Minister under the Office of the Permanent Secretary in 1989. It is a large organization with over fifty employees and an advisory board with many members. As the most active member of the advisory board and a veteran of government affairs, Dr. Saisuree Chutikul unofficially heads the agency and supervises the employees. Dr. Saisuree often solicits cooperation and involvement from women-centered NGOs (often excluding the GDRI), and she mobilizes cooperation between NGOs. "We can't work alone," she explained, "so we always invite NGOs. Sometimes they advise on a personal or professional basis." Since the National Commission On Women's Affairs is a government agency, they only operate between the hours of 8:30 and 4:30. "When you want to change something," Dr. Saisuree complained, "it's like a slow boat to China" (Chutikul, personal interview, 1995). NGOs can work twenty-four hours a day, so their participation accelerates the process and provides additional support. It also forces the government, often dismissive, to acknowledge the presence of these NGOs, increasing the possibility that it will address their concerns.

While Dr. Saisuree Chutikul supervised most projects, she did not hold veto power or exercise complete control. For example, despite her refusal to support an expensive publication entitled *Thai Women*, ten thousand copies of the book were printed for official distribution. These copies were presented to people and institutions in Thailand as gifts, generating no income despite their significant production cost. The book highlighted the work done by royal and titled women of Thailand. *Thai Women* offered a superficial history of what is called "The Heritage of Thai Women" and celebrated the achievements of prominent, wealthy, upper-class women such as the Queen, Royal Ladies, "Decorated Women Active in Community Service," and "Prominent Government Officials and Women Leaders in the Provinces."

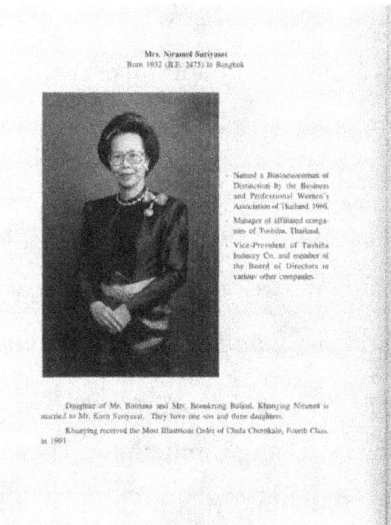

Image 4.4 and Image 4.5

These women were pictured decorated in finery, and their family connections and achievements were documented in detail. Dr. Saisuree has noted that all of the women presented in this publication have already received recognition for their work, and there has been no international interest expressed in publications of this kind. The book merely celebrates the lives of the elite. The money for the publication could have been used to reward more industrious women, to acknowledge the achievements of women from less privileged backgrounds, or to produce a publication aimed at attracting international support. Despite her disapproval, the book was published and disseminated to foreign government officials and businesses involved in Thai joint ventures. Dr. Saisuree assumed they were not read as she received no comments from the recipients.

After the book was distributed, the GDRI produced a modest publication entitled *Profile of Women in Thailand*. Written in both English and Thai using funds from the Ford Foundation, it provided statistics about the situation of all women in Thailand. *Profile* charted the improvements in the past two decades for women in the areas of health, education, employment, and income as well as the increase in opportunities for economic, social, and political participation. The positions held by women were also compared to those of men, revealing women's continued subordinate status in development and politics. Ninety-two tables and charts in this eighty-page document provided detailed statististics that supported the *Profile's* narrative. Graphics included boxed sections called "Highlights," and the numbered chapters and sections reflect a common western-style, social science format that gives the report empirical authority. Most documents produced by the Gender and Development Research Institute are inexpensively produced, easily available for purchase, and follow this social science format that lends credibility to its assessments. Projects of this sort make the GDRI appear much more focused and effective.

Dr. Suteera Thomson, educated in the west—she received her Ph.D. in Canada—and married to a *farang*, operates her NGO differently than other women-centered NGOs in Bangkok. Her professional, output-oriented GDRI, also referred to as the "Association for the Promotion of the Status of Women," explicitly supports Women In Development (WID) projects. She successfully solicited funds from many institutions outside of Thailand, ensuring that the GDRI maintained exclusive managerial and financial control of their Thailand-based projects. For example, in coordination with the German humanitarian foundation Friedrich Ebert Stiftung, the GDRI sponsored the establishment and maintenance of regional Gender Watch Groups (GWG) that organized meetings, conferences, and discussions and charted regional promotion and awareness of gender related issues throughout Thailand. They also monitored the implementation of policies on women's issues formulated by regional and provincial political parties. The Asia Foundation provided financial support for the Gender Watch Group's biannual English language *GWG Newsletter*. This newsletter reported on the promotion of the roles and the status of women in national and regional development. By diversifying its sources of funding, the GDRI maintained primary control, limiting its need to justify expenditures to contributors and enabling it to choose which projects within Thailand it would launch. For their participation, contributors received GDRI's extensive English-language publications.

These documents reported gender inequities that persisted in Thailand and assessed the projects carried out by the organization. They invariably described successes in these professional presentations, including supporting evidence in the form of tables, charts, and graphs. Because Dr. Suteera presented timely, social science style reports of successful WID promoting projects, she was able to justify her control over the way in which international funds were used. Dr. Thomson believed that her international donors felt confident that their money was well spent and working toward development, alleviating her accountability and the pressure to conduct projects according to the opinions or requests of external funders. (Thomas, personal interview, 1995).

The GDRI also secured its influential position by efficiently responding to the needs of the Thai Government. After the NGO conference in Beijing, the GDRI offered to help the government produce a plan to promote gender equity. The National Commission On Women's Affairs, an arm of the national Thai government, saw this as encroaching on its responsibilities. Over the years, a rivalry has developed between the woman who runs this government-sponsored organization, Dr. Saisuree, and Dr. Suteera. Dr. Suteera's organization was perceived by the National Commission to be aggressive self-promotion that violated Thai rules of conduct (Saisuree, personal interview, 1995). Although Dr. Suteera ignored Thai etiquette, her timely, professional reputation led to a decision by members of the Thai Government to commission and pay the GDRI for several projects rather than the National Commission, which was, indeed, the government branch designed to conduct these projects. The GDRI was chosen particularly when the assignment would reach international audiences (Thomas, personal interview, 1995). Increasingly, manners and earlier protocol became less important as focus shifted beyond Thai borders.

Image 4.6

The GDRI regularly publishes and disseminates statistics-based research reports in both Thai and English to local and international audiences. The slick, professional publications, her finesse at securing outside funding, and the promotion of WID strategies developed in the first world that privileged a prescribed path toward industrial development rendered Dr. Suteera the object of criticism by other women-centered groups. Yet her productivity and the control she maintained over the organization were admired. Her opinions consistently determined how projects will be carried out. For example, when the majority of photographs submitted to the first annual "Women and Work" photograph contest sponsored by the GDRI were, as Dr. Suteera explained, romanticized images of rural Thai women taking care of children or cooking for their families, she chose to ignore these entries (personal interview, 1995). Rather than judging the photographs according to technical or aesthetic considerations, the few photographs that veered from the rural-women-as-mothers theme were pronounced the winners. Accordingly, the submissions in the year that followed reflected women at work, the theme that Dr. Suteera was interested in promoting. Prizes were awarded to the photographs representing women involved in non-traditional occupations. In subsequent years, the photographs submitted increasingly reflect the themes proffered by Dr. Suteera. The winners in 1995 included an old woman throwing pots in a factory called "Pots for Sale," women construction workers working at high altitudes called "Dangerous Work," (see image 4.6) a woman operating a large, but delicate, machine entitled "Women and Technology," a woman using a hand held sanding device on intricate metalwork entitled "Finishing Touch," and a women in a rubber forest using a hand-operated press to produce rubber entitled "Producing Rubber Sheet." After the promotion of development was established, some photographs were chosen that illustrated increased gender equality outside of industry—a woman with a paintbrush seated in an ornate temple entitled "Painting Thai Design" and teenagers marching while playing tubas called "Blowing while Carrying." The 1995 images portrayed both expected women's occupations in industrial Thailand—making pots, doing construction, producing rubber, mending fishnet—and activities usually reserved for men—artwork for temples, working with technology, and playing tubas. In addition, the ages, styles of dress, and ethnicities of the women varied; and the photographs are well-executed, colorful, and striking in composition.

Each of the organizations that I have discussed presents stereotypical images of Thai women to non-Thais. Rather than producing and disseminating images of Thai women as sex-workers or wives, a prevalent stereotype I address in Chapter Five, they provided alternative romanticized female images, yet their strategy for representation still followed the previous international trajectory. This practice garnered international attention by using recent technologies to produce and distribute a variety of texts that exploited the humanist doctrine that each individual possesses certain rights. In the attempt to alter Thailand's national image, improve the status of Thai women, and gain international support for their projects, these NGOs extended the metaphoric link between the Thai nation and Thai women, circulating new idealized depictions of Thai women that can resonate with the beliefs and values of their non-Thai audience.

EMPOWERing Sex-Workers

This final section considers another Thai NGO that interacts with previous depictions of women; but rather than shifting or extending the types of images circulating that exploit the predominant international stereotype of Thai woman as sex-worker. EMPOWER was one of the first organizations to posit sex-work as part of an entertainment industry, promoting education and alliance in order to diminish the shame associated with this profession. EMPOWER encouraged Thai sex-workers to take control of interpretations about their lives and produce their own representations for western men in Thailand, especially those who enjoy their services.

Before 2000, there were no Thai-originated NGOs that explicitly tried to end prostitution in Thailand. Sex-work is unofficially recognized by the government as essential to tourism. Brothel owners are rich and powerful, and many tourists, as well as Thai men, participate in this economy, so that such an agency would face strong opposition from many sources both inside and outside Thailand. In response to international feminist outcries against sexual exploitation, however, several NGOs attempting to end child prostitution and international traffic of women were established. Headquartered in Bangkok with branches in Sri Lanka, Taiwan, and the Philippines, ECPAT (End Child Prostitution in Asian Tourism) was an NGO dedicated to eliminating the sexual exploitation of Asian children by foreign men. The Foundation for Women (FFW) also addressed child prostitution by creating a series of children's storybooks about a young girl from rural Thailand named Kamla who, as a result of a series of unfortunate events, moves to Bangkok and becomes a sex-worker. These books were distributed to rural schools in an attempt to educate children about the dangers of sex-work. Written and circulated throughout Thailand in Thai, they have been reproduced in an English language translation so that the FFW can share strategies and participate in international discussions. ECPAT and FFW similarly addressed both Thai and international audiences in their attempt to dismantle the international traffic of Thai women using education and legal intervention through the application of universally accepted laws.

EMPOWER (Education Means Protection of Women Engaged in Recreation), founded in 1985, was Thailand's sole NGO dedicated to educating adult Thai sex-workers. Initially targeting women employed at the brothels of Bangkok's Patpong, the notorious red light district designed to attract *farang* (and other non-Thai) tourists, its target population broadened to include Thai gay men and *kathoeys* involved in the sex industry and Thai sex-workers who work with both Thai and non-Thai customers. Successful in generating funds and attracting sex-worker participation, it expanded, adding a branch in the suburbs and another in Thailand's second largest city, Chiang Mai. As opposed to positing the end of prostitution as their goal, EMPOWER provided skills training, thereby increasing the self-esteem of sex-workers. These skills taught by EMPOWER encouraged women who provide recreational services to expand their possibilities for employment and to understand and respond to injustices that they experienced. Most bar owners tolerated, and sometimes even condoned, their employees' participation because more confident women with better language abilities could enhance bar profits. However, other NGOs criticized EMPOWER for several reasons. Thai studies scholar Nerida Cook reports on the position held by EMPOWER compared with other Thai women-centered NGOs:

> As a result of its unusual perspective, EMPOWER finds itself criticised for its stance towards prostitution (in that support is taken to imply legitimisation). Other women's groups also feel distanced by EMPOWER activists' lack of involvement in the more mainstream women's movement (Tantiwiramanond and Pandey, 1991, p. 133). . . . It would appear that the workers of EMPOWER, in dealing closely with prostitutes, and in refusing to maintain a core element of the more usual middle-class women's position of outright rejection of prostitution as a choice, have become marginalised from their own social group. Programmes for prostitutes appear more socially acceptable when oriented to assisting women to leave prostitution. (Cook, 1998, pp. 275-76)

Cook accurately assessed the way in which EMPOWER's mission diverges from those of other Thai NGOs. EMPOWER was also unique in its efforts to provide its target population with the means for generating their own English language representations as opposed to producing them on their behalf in order to garner international support. EMPOWER's founder and leader, Chantawipa Apisuk, provided occasional interviews to non-

Thai organizations or researchers, yet EMPOWER itself did not produce extensive English-language texts. In 1996, its English language materials, all available for purchase, consisted of a video that described its programs and showed its facilities (created by Christian Aid in 1992), a single-page brochure outlining their mission, and pins and T-shirts emblazoned with EMPOWER's name. By enabling English language communication, the production of representations by their participants, encouraging each sex-worker to follow her own agenda, EMPOWER puts the language in the hands of those they represent and teach. And these sex-workers are encouraged to converse with their customers rather than the Thai government or international funding organizations.

In order to do this, EMPOWER continually conducted free English classes that emphasized AIDS awareness. Tantiwiramanond and Pandey have explained the benefits of learning English:

> A grasp of English is a necessity for the women because most foreign customers of Thai bar workers speak English, especially in the Patpong area. Knowing English helps these women to avoid exploitation. Without the ability to communicate with customers they can be easily conned. When choices of jobs are limited and wages are insecure, language training opens up the possibility of other employment. English classes also provide a medium where women from different bars can sit together and discuss their feelings, their work and problems. Together in a classroom, women begin to feel that they are not alone. (Tantiwiramanond, 1991, pp. 131-2)

Many women working in this industry stopped school at the fourth grade level, so these classes refamiliarized them with techniques for learning, and as their language skills improved, provided them with a sense of accomplishment. They were also encouraged to form a community premised on learning and achievement. Furthermore, learning English enabled the bar workers to communicate effectively with their customers, making them more valuable employees positioned to request better conditions from their employers. Increasingly able to negotiate with their clients for better compensation and for protection from exposure to HIV, these sex-workers could become more confident and better able to improve their situations.

EMPOWER offered many programs between 1985 and 2012 that shifted according to the skills possessed by volunteers and the availability of funding. Until 2004, EMPOWER, in conjunction with the government-sponsored Continuing Education department, provided instruction and guidance for the completion of elementary, junior high, and high school level workbooks. Completion of these courses qualified participants to take state administered examinations that grant diplomas to those who pass. These diplomas enabled women to compete for jobs that do not involve sex-work or assembly-line manufacturing. Women at EMPOWER who passed these exams were encouraged to tutor or teach those who were in the preparatory stages. This facilitated community formation among EMPOWER participants and provided experience in the highly esteemed profession of teaching. EMPOWER volunteers also provided translation and transcription services, supporting English-language correspondence between sex-workers and their clients who have left Thailand. In addition, training programs such as clothing manufacture and design, as well as additional language training in Japanese, French, or German were offered regularly. Participants expressed themselves through sewing, drawing, magazine production, batik, and in street theater through EMPOWER's popular drama. Batiks were painted on T-shirts and banners to represent EMPOWER. Plays written by participants in both Thai and English were regularly performed at conventions involving EMPOWER, and annually at a Bangkok theatre for interested guests. On the streets of Patpong, the infamous sex tourism area, street theater productions occasionally disrupted the bar area. Often the actors were taking time off from working in these same bars to perform this guerilla theater for the unexpecting audiences they would normally serve. Between 1986 and 2001, EMPOWER members, volunteers and students together, produced 46 Thai-English language newsletters (*Patpong* and *Empower)* that were distributed in bars to clients or other sex-workers. Once or twice a year, a trip was coordinated; for a nominal fee, participants were invited on all expense paid retreat, normally beach side, complete with games and activities that build confidence, trust, and a sense of community.

Teaching done at EMPOWER was responsive to the interests of the participants. While discussions about sexual anatomy and sex acts were taboo among Thai women—even sex-workers—when speaking in Thai,[66] English classes at EMPOWER could be sexually explicit.

---

66 One student threatened to hit me if I said "koiay" again (Thai word for penis) and told me to call all sexually related body parts "inside stuff."

I volunteered there from 1995-1996 and was asked to teach English classes. These classes were not to have lesson plans but, instead, I was to teach what the students attending each class requested to learn. During one of my lessons, the students asked about the appropriate use of terms such as penis, and vagina, as opposed to "cock" and "pussy." Even the women who were not sex-workers were extremely interested. They asked other questions about the meanings of words beyond the obvious (for example, having a headache suggesting not wanting sex or having a backache as a hint for a massage). These words and phrases required cultural and contextual knowledge not easily obtained, yet they were used frequently by customers of these working students. And EMPOWER's aim was to provide them with literacy that served the students. After starting another class about clothes and colors, the students showed me a handout they received from another instructor the previous day entitled "What's Fair." It contained dialogues that subverted potentially exploitative situations. One student said to me, "I work in the bar and need to understand what the customers are saying to me, not the stuff you're teaching us now." I modified my subject matter accordingly, extending the previous day's discussion that included phrases suitable to improving their communication at work such as, "You lied to me so now I can't believe you;" "I've been worried about you;" and "I fall in love slowly because I want to be sure I'm not making a mistake." The participants told me what to teach them, asking me to explain the meaning of words and then construct sentences containing these words. Students seized the opportunity to learn those aspects of the English language meaningful to them in order to establish dialogues with clients.

They actively pursued knowledge of English so that they could control the representations they generated and gauge their reception. The ability to communicate in English increased the control these women have in their participation in international markets.

Classes, performances, and publications encouraged the people who came to EMPOWER to express themselves in their own voices. Tantiwiramanond and Pandey have the following appraisal of EMPOWER:

> EMPOWER is a unique grass roots effort mostly carried out by bar girls of the Patpong area for their own upliftment. Both the annual drama show, which attracts a good-sized crowd in Bangkok, and its newspaper have helped the women to project themselves as workers in need of understanding and better working conditions. (Tantiwiramanond, 1991, p. 133)

The presence of these classes, shows, and publications affect both the producers and their audience, which includes Thai nationals and many kinds of visitors from nations around the world.

In 2012, Empower reformed as an organization and had a workshop, art show, and publication based on an extended study they had conducted about sex work and human trafficking. Women involved in the sex work industry were interviewed as well as provided the resources to use storytelling and cloth images to show that human trafficking laws actually present a double bind for sex-workers by allowing police and NGOs to define exploitation in ways that violated the basic human rights of sex workers. The report, the art, and the speeches clearly redefine lack of agency involved in victimizing rhetorics of the UN as well as the ways exploitation is defined counter to the interests of those trafficked it seeks to protect. The ways in which these laws are deployed do not serve Thai sex work populations and this is rendered visible through Empower's report ("Hit and Run," 2012).

While Thai sex-workers are often assumed to have no voice in an international context, the increasing number of conversations that take place within Thailand with *farang* affects their image beyond the confines of their nation. Rather than relying on NGO employees to speak on their behalf, all women who participate in the activities of EMPOWER must generate representations in English that take into account current global conditions, imported belief systems and the way in which each of these factors are played out in Bangkok. As their knowledge increases, these women make more informed decisions about which strategies create the effects they desire.

Rather than responding to a dynamic global environment by simply adopting western articles and customs that I considered earlier, the NGOs I studied used new technologies such as state of the art printing and information dispersal, internet and digital communication, audience-specific language use, and creative, flexible and responsive knowledge dispersal techniques for informing, teaching and learning, in addition to invoking western humanist doctrines in their attempt to effect changes and acquire international support. By exploiting the new media developments of the time as quickly as they developed, these NGOs effectively used rhetoric and representations that extended beyond mere translation, with a nuanced invocation of both Thai and western ideologies. In a manner similar to the way Sadie Plant feminizes computer development by linking it to weaving, EMPOWER brought the weaving of cloth to expose subtle intricacies inherent in western human rights discourses. EMPOWER has its constituency speak for themselves, from whatever perspective they wish. Other Thai NGOs discussed in this chapter use other strategies to speak on behalf of Thai women. Each of these Thai NGOs can be credited with feminizing the processes of globalization by using cutting-edge technologies, innovative content delivery, and cross cultural literacy to establish international platforms upon which to pursue their projects.

The representations produced by Thai women-centered NGOs and the National Commission On Women's Affairs use many tactics to achieve their goals. Despite their different practices and agendas, however, they each succeed not only in responding to their contemporary global environment but also in helping to shape the way gender, class, ethnicity, and nation are being understood within Thailand and in the evolving global public sphere. Nerida Cook concluded her essay, "Thailand: 'Dutiful Daughters,' Estranged Sisters," hoping we can "begin to understand the ways in which [Thai middle-class women] are defining their own sexuality and class identity in the context of middle-class experience and global feminist discourses" (1998, p. 279). This chapter suggests that Thai women-centered NGOs are defining themselves not only "in the context of" but also *in their construction of* global feminist discourses.

5

Stereotypes and Rice

Images of Thailand as an exotic, erotic destination where beautiful women eagerly await to serve and satisfy western men are pervasive in the western media. In *Night Market: Sexual Cultures and the Thai Economic Miracle*, Ryan Bishop and Lillian S. Robinson asserted, "[t]he stereotype of Thailand as the playground of the Western World dominates the public imagination outside the country and is continually reiterated in the popular media" (1998, p.16). Most representations of Thailand that circulate outside of Thailand depict Thai women in two categories: exotic, young, alluring, yet potentially HIV-positive "hookers," eager to please western clients, or dutiful, devoted wives of western men who dismiss the tenets of western feminism and appreciate the financial and emotional generosity of their husbands. In both instances, Thai women appear happily subservient to western men. Bishop and Robinson prove, through meticulous archival work, that these images have dominated international media since the Vietnam War. And contemporary non-Thai media continue their proliferation, limiting coverage of Thailand almost exclusively to Thai prostitution and mail order brides. Bishop and Robinson wrote, "Perhaps the matter is one not of quantity but of focus. Thailand is, in fact, conspicuous by its presence in the popular media. So Thailand *is* a story, but audiences always receive the same story" (1998, p. 53). Only since July 1997 when Thailand allowed its currency to float freely in international markets causing massive devaluation, have media considerations expanded to include the Thai nation as the instigator of the Asian Financial Crisis.[67] Yet these two categories of Thai women still dominate the non-Thai television and print media considerations of Thailand. As a result, these images possess a global reality effect beyond Thailand's borders.

What Bishop and Ryan call the "story" of Thailand affects the assumptions of more than the armchair newsreader. Returning after my first year in Thailand, I was repeatedly queried by my family and friends—for whom Thailand had existed for more than a year as a country where someone they knew lived and worked—about whether the sex market was as wild as they had heard. Stubbornly, I told them that was not the object of my fieldwork, despite its sex and gender orientation. Much, I said often, is written on this topic: I described my research about the roles of English-language terms for sex and gender that are deployed by

---

67 While Thailand is occasionally referred to as an "Economic Miracle," or, since October 1997, as the country that triggered the Southeast Asian financial crisis, these economic images still recycle gendered images. Boonchalaksi and Guest explain economic growth in terms of the commercialization of Thai women's sexuality: "The bodies of Thai women have become one of the bases of growth of the Thai economy" (1994, p. 1).

Thais in Bangkok to enhance their understanding of their own sexualities and genders rather than to replicate our general sense of these words. Despite this, professors, graduate students, friends, and acquaintances repeatedly presumed that the ethnographic studies you have just read centered on sex-workers and the sex trade. After submitting an essay about self-identified gay Thai men in Bangkok to two journals, the five anonymous readers unanimously suggested that I include a discussion of Thai women who participate in the sex-work industry. To me, this was absurdly off topic, but to readers only familiar with western-generated popular press about Thailand, any discussion of sex and/or sexuality seemed incomplete without being placed within the context of the infamous sex-work industry. The pervasiveness of this discourse is evident from the cover of Ryan and Bishop's book that features a photograph of Thai women seated in a brothel display window. This picture occupies more than half of the cover despite Bishop and Ryan's thesis, an extended critique of the persistent yoking of Thai sex-workers in the western media's portrayal of Thailand. Thus even in the act of critique, these stereotypes resonate through their relentless repetition in different arenas.

New generalizations are emerging constantly, and they differ according to the population. In August and September 2012, I conducted a brief poll of fifty Chicago residents over the age of 30 asking them what words they think of that are associated with Thailand. Over half of my respondents described Thailand as a corrupt country replete with drugged children that are sex slaves.[68] Yet this was not the

68 This is a result of the western media attention paid to the arrest of

only association. All but one participant cited Thai food. In addition, Thailand conjured beaches, vacation destinations, partying, recreational drug use (the film *Hangover 2* was cited by six respondents), prostitution, child prostitution, and government corruption. Repeatedly, respondents that mentioned "undeveloped" and "poverty" also associated Thailand with high-tech designer knock-offs and inexpensive, cutting-edge luxury goods. Transgendered people or "Lady-boys," Tuk-tuks, and Muay Thai Boxing were mentioned by eight of the thirty respondents.

Competing images enable us to realize that gender and sex are not simple, fixed, nor timeless. And the meanings attached to gender and sex change—not only in cultural comparisons such as "west" versus "Thai," but within groups that inhabit the same city at the same time as well as about certain groups in international arenas. The latter will be the subject of this final chapter: pernicious stereotypes of Thais in international arenas and how their circulation with additional images dilutes their pervasive power. I will examine images circulated by Thailand on the Internet, as well as cultural and local examples that may serve to stimulate new ways of dynamic thinking about the import and export of language.

Exotic Travel

Thailand is no longer simply a destination for western men to

---

westerners in Thailand. Thai laws are very strict concerning pederasty. While child abuse occurs in the US, a western arrested in Thailand for child prostitution makes more sensational headlines than one occurring domestically. Thus the information circulating is far greater, while actual incidents of child prostitution or child abuse may not be substantially different.

find wives and prostitutes. Nor do visitors expect to see desperate drug-addled children filling the streets. As the western perspective becomes increasingly transnational through economic and media exposure, Thailand's beautiful beaches, extravagant hotels, superb cuisine, and exotic landscape have produced competing images as a haven for both elite tourists and budget travelers. Medical tourism is also becoming part of the vacation images associated with Thailand. Thus, rather than focusing on debunking the sex-work myth, exposing more of Thailand and circulating more images, ideas, and information, has provided the key to weakening this enduring trope.

Since the Vietnam War, Thailand has been depicted as a vacation paradise for westerners. Initially, known for sex tourism, Thailand's tourism industry recast itself between the 1970s and 1990s as becoming the next most profitable industry. The Tourism Authority of Thailand, along with other Thai and non-Thai tourist agencies crafted increasingly diverse tour packages. Thailand was presented as a welcoming culture—the Land of Smiles—offering a myriad of tourist packages as the industry grew (Image 5.1).

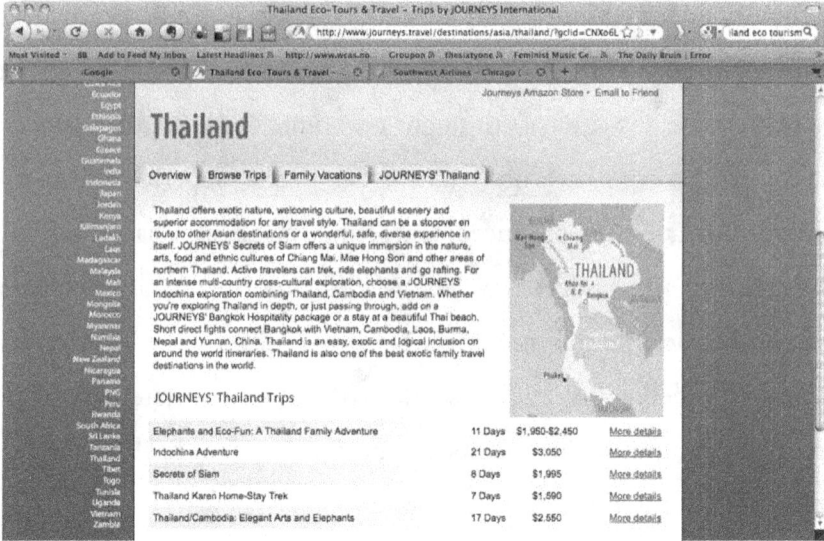

Image 5.1

Until the end of the twentieth-century, international travel agencies offering packages to visit Thailand were used more often than Thailand-based tourist agencies, even though Thailand-based tourist businesses advertised to non-Thai clientele in English (as well as German, French, and Japanese). Before 1998, no sites promoted Thailand as a medical tourist destination, and only a few Thailand-based sites did so after 1998[69] In the late 1990s, Malaysia was the first non-European or U.S. country to promote medical tourism online. Thailand's online tourism offerings bloomed from the sex trade to business and family travel. With the founding of the Tourism Authority of Thailand in 1960, the country was dubbed "Exotic Thailand" and "The Land of Smiles," and, in 2010, "Amazing Thailand." Internet-based marketing reached beyond backpack travellers to professional travelers, offering luxurious

69 This is based on hits. Thus an international travel agency like Travelocity, American Express, or Thomas Cook, Ltd might have had more traffic because they offered services to other countries as well as Thailand.

hotels and meeting centers as well as upscale and typically western vacation activities such as golf, fishing, and fine dining. Family vacation packages touted beautiful Buddhist monuments and natural sights in a safe and friendly environment. These online travel packages morphed after 1994 from all-inclusive "See Exotic Thailand" trips to more specifically targeted and themed packages like jungle and eco tours or meditation and Thai yoga retreats. According to the 2003-2013 "Policy and Marketing Plan" of the Tourism Authority of Thailand, the internet afforded the chance for Thai-generated tourist operators, supported by the state-led campaign, to reach western audiences with English-language offers of historical tours, luxury hotel hopping and world class shopping, adventure sporting, Thai boxing and other spectator sports directed at different upscale niches attracting a broad range of tourists.

Thai tourism not only targeted business luxury, national monuments, and Thai sports; packages emerged offering unique cross-cultural experiences for religious education, remote wildlife tours, and encounters with indigenous tribes people. The multiplication of five-star accommodations expanded, as did new package themes including: relaxation and meditation, or learning Thai massage. Families were invited to Thailand to enjoy elephant rides, and eco-tourism was created for environmentally conscientious travelers interested in comfort yet wishing to make a small environmental footprint.

Thai uses of web marketing have been strong and persistent since tourism became an Internet commodity. While Thailand is well known for sex tours, it has also consistently marketed to tourists the potential for transformation—mental and physical modifications produced through travel by interacting with Thais, their traditions, culture, and territory. Not only did Thailand tourism offer relaxation and service on their websites created by Thai tourist agencies, but western—and particularly European—countries presented exoticism, particularly service-oriented, as an implicit feature of the myriad of tourist experiences available in Thailand.

Following the 1997 economic crisis, the government of Thailand endorsed medical tourism. It has since become an increasingly visible offering on the web; new sites dedicated to medical tourism have emerged—based either within or outside of Thailand.[70] The most notable shift in online marketing for tourism to Thailand is the addition of Sexual Reassignment Surgeries (SRS) as a potential destination. Not only have SRS-specific websites in English been undergoing rapid change, so have the websites set up by the most prominent cosmetic surgery hospitals catering to western tourists as well as to upper-class Thais within Thailand.

The Landscape of Thailand's Medical Industry

There is a long history of surgery, particularly cosmetic surgery, practiced in Thailand. Thailand offers high quality hospitals, western-educated doctors, and cutting-edge technologies, all for comparatively inexpensive procedures. Cosmetic surgery in the United States means many things from facelifts to breast enhancements to tummy tucks. However, in Thailand, each surgeon has expertise in one or two particular

---

70 As noted in Bookman and Bookman (2007).

surgeries, and as a result, has vast experience over time in performing these surgeries. Thai surgeons, as opposed to western-based cosmetic practitioners, are expected to be highly competent and experienced in only one very specific area. Cosmetic surgery in Thailand was considered elective, socially acceptable, and consumer-oriented. Hospital websites, such as Yanhee, offered statistics about where doctors were educated, how many surgeries they had done, what particular surgeries they had completed, and whether or not the surgeries were considered successful. As consumers with choices in surgeons, surgical locations, and armed with price information, and analysis of doctors' education, skills, and success, patients would generally undergo a single surgery at a time. Yanhee Hospital has different floors equipped for and dedicated to nose reconstruction or eye surgery.

Westerners within Thailand are always considered tourists and foreigners. Even with new visa restrictions for retirees who choose to live in Thailand, the Thai government requires that all foreigners not having specific work or study visas renew their status every ninety days. Renewal used to require leaving the country to obtain a fresh stamp upon return, but now one must merely visit a desk in a hospital or local government office to renew status. The practice of keeping even permanently residing foreigners registering helps maintain the idea that non-Thais are never really Thai residents. As a result, the medical tourism industry appears much larger than it actually is: all foreigners receiving any kind of medical attention are considered medical tourists.

That being the case, initially the outward face of websites did not need to cater to non-local desires. Westerners within Thailand are not likely to adopt Thai notions of sex, gender, or sexuality exposed to them on a daily basis: most foreigners within Thailand speak only rudimentary Thai, and their lives are not disrupted by their location. Thai nationals tend to accept western presumptions and expectations at face value, not requiring that they follow local customs but appreciating when they do. Bangkok seems like a western city with exotic sights to an expatriate who wishes verisimilitude and familiarity abroad. Moreover, hospitals and clinics operate with English staff, so expatriates expect English—even if it is grammatically imperfect and not prone to illustrating or explaining Thai worldviews.

A significant asset of the Thai surgical practice is the competence and experience of Thai doctors. Thai surgeons educated and practicing in Bangkok and other large places have, in fact, far more surgical experience than most of their western counterparts. While most cosmetic surgery in the U.S. is very expensive and requires a fixed set of surgical methods, Thai surgeons are free to practice their expertise without government and insurance company oversight. Historically, the most prominent Thai surgeons attended medical schools in western countries, but for several decades Thai medical schools have offered excellent educations with cutting-edge medical technologies and educational material, which was imported from the U.S. and U.K. As a result, all doctors in Thailand could speak impeccable English when discussing medical procedures and ideas, even if they had done their training in Thailand.

Yanhee Plastic Surgeons		
Dr. Somsak Chuleewattanapong **Languages Spoken**: Thai, English » More information YANHEE HOSPITAL	Number of Cases Performed	Cases
	Augmentation Rhinoplasty	1,200 cases
	Upper Blepharoplasty/Double Eyelid	800 cases
	Lower Blepharoplasty	700 cases
	Alarplasty	700 cases
	Augmentation Mammoplasty	500 cases
	Liposuction	500 cases
	Botox Injection	500 cases
	Mentopalsty	300 cases
	Mid-Facelift	200 cases
	Etc	2,440 cases
Dr. Pitch Paiboonkasemsutthi **Languages Spoken**: Thai, English » More information YANHEE HOSPITAL	Number of Cases Performed	Cases
	Augmentation Rhinoplasty	7,300 cases
	Upper Blepharoplasty/Double Eyelid	6,300 cases
	Lower Blepharoplasty	5,400 cases
	Alarplasty	3,000 cases
	Augmentation Mammoplasty	2,400 cases
	Liposuction	1,400 cases
	Botox Injection	850 cases
	Lipofilling	800 cases
	Tummy Tuck	710 cases
	Etc	5,560 cases
Dr. Thawatchai Boonpadhanapong, **Languages Spoken**: Thai, English	Number of Cases Performed	Cases
	Augmentation Rhinoplasty	2,000 cases
	Botox Injection	1,500 cases
	Lower Blepharoplasty	1,200 cases
	Upper Blepharoplasty/Double Eyelid	1,200 cases
	Alarplasty	1,000 cases

Image 5.2

As a result of specialization, as well as widespread social acceptance of cosmetic surgery procedures and significantly lower costs, and few government or insurance regulations, Thai surgeons may hone a single craft and practice it many more times annually than a U.S. surgeon may practice in a career. As a result of specialization, widespread social acceptance, significantly lower costs, and not government or insurance regulations, Thai surgeons may hone a single craft and practice it many more times annually than a U.S. surgeon. Accordingly, doctors in Thailand are expected to keep track of their surgeries and their results. Hospitals maintain a list of doctors, their photographs, and the surgeries they have performed. Such lists are still available in Thai directly from the hospitals, but they are no longer updated in English. For example, some surgeons at Yanhee Hospital have completed 7,000 to 9,000 surgeries of a single process. (See Image 5.2)

Patients are expected to purchase exactly what they want—single procedures from the doctor of their choice. Thus one cosmetic surgery package may consist of numerous procedures, such as skin tightening, nose reconstruction, and saline injection, and each surgery package might have a different doctor execute each procedure. Customers could go to hospital databanks or websites and choose a doctor based on price, experience, hospital location, and time constraints. For cosmetic nose surgery, a Thai patient could show up in the morning, take any surgeon available, pay the advertised price, complete the surgery, and leave by dinnertime. A phone call or online registration was enough to book a procedure and payment was expected upon hospital entry. Prices for these surgeries are much lower in Thailand than the comparatively high western standards for "elective" procedures. Prices were kept modest to remain within reach of the largest customer base, even without insurance coverage.

Thailand has expert plastic surgery—more sexual reassignment surgeries take place in Bangkok alone than any other country, yet sex reassignment *tout court* is not the goal of most hospital visitors. Instead, Thais choose how, when, and where to transition and what requires modification—in line with their specific conceptions of desire as well as their pocketbooks. Most patients do not go to these hospitals to transition from one sex or one gender or one ethnicity (here I am referencing eyelid surgery), reproductive state (such as pregnancy through reproductive technologies), or youth preservation (such as facial reconstruction).

Transition instead takes many forms and suggests a multiple range of trajectories with or without endpoints.

In the past several decades, Thailand's image in the U.S. has shifted to one more prevalent among the traveling community—largely European, but also business elite and backpack trekkers who take time to explore the world. This image circulated more forcefully in the past in Europe, Japan, Singapore, and other prosperous Asian nations, but it now is a competing trope for U.S. globetrotters. Thailand's tourist industry had increased exponentially, expanding in the 70s and accelerating since this study. Tourism, not rice, is now the leading industry for the country. Income from tourism far exceeds all other exports and is a large indicator of the country's health and GNP. The Tourism Authority of Thailand (TAT) has successfully permeated the international market with its promotion of Thailand as "The Land of Smiles" and "Amazing Thailand." The smiling, friendly population has infiltrated the collective U.S. imagination long enough to shift the stage, existing alongside and for certain audiences, joining the already existing vocabularies.

These websites, which emerge at an exponential rate and appear as top hits in non-Thailand-related searches concerning gender and sex surgery, are creating an industry involving thousands of Thai and Western visitors annually. Because the growth of modern medical travel has developed subsequent to the establishment of the Internet as a travel information source, the foundation of medical facilitation is fundamentally an online presence. Consequently, medical tourism marketed through the Internet, where initial contact takes place via the web, has become a staple for people seeking information concerning sex/gender related surgeries in any location. For a potential patient interested in these medical procedures, there are few other sources of information available. Even workers in the U.S. medical community remain unknowledgeable of the rudimentary basics of medical tourism. With titles such as *The Complete Idiot's Guide to Medical Tourism* (2009) and *Beauty from Afar* (2006), printed guides are not notable resources for cosmetic surgery abroad. Thus the Internet is the primary source for cosmetic surgery through medical tourism. Thailand is present wherever a search on cosmetic surgery, gender reassignment surgery, or medical tourism is entered into a major search engine regardless of location.

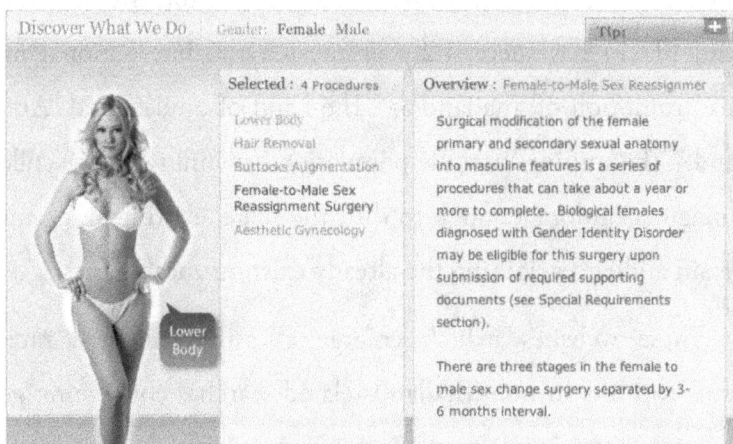

Image 5.3

The integrative nature of online consumerism has driven growth and expansion of Thailand's medical tourism industry. Thai websites for cosmetic surgery travel, particularly SRS, reach out to web surfers through their ubiquitous wired technology and interpolate them as potential customers. "One-click" shoppers now have the potential to book medical vacations—including SRS—to Thailand in under 24 hours. Every business day marks an online expansion of the medical tourism industry and Thailand is present whenever travel and surgery are invoked. As web technology is now ubiquitous through access on an array of mobile devices, and always available in places that a decade ago seemed off the grid. Before the 20th century, Thailand did not appear as a place for excellent surgical procedures. Yet through web marketing this expertise, and constant access to this information by interested users of technology outside of Thailand, its virtual presence has allowed it to reach page visitors outside of Thailand and promote medical tourism. By tracking page choice and time spent on particular websites, which are monitored constantly, webmasters can engage virtual visitors through chat bubbles, pop-up windows, or special offers, to enter into dialogue with Thai operators. When a browser window rests on surgery websites for a significant time, or hits a number of interconnected websites, the person at the screen, regardless of location, is greeted as an individual by a personal receptionist in Thailand ready to text, chat, or talk by phone. In the past two years voluntary surgery has become intricately linked to the nation of Thailand, and this association will surely grow stronger and more pervasive.

Thus the Thai SRS industry online and the recent proliferation of medical tourist site aggregators are offering a new version of Thailand as a medical destination. This image is strong; when you search online for cosmetic surgery or Gender Reassignment Surgery or Sexual

Reassignment Surgery in the U.S., Thai surgery sites are one of the top hits. The foregrounding of safe, advanced, fast, and customer-endorsed Gender Reassignment Surgery illustrates that the technologies of Thailand, as a medical hub for westerners, has emerged as a site for SRS-related medical tourism, attracting SRS patients to Thailand. This evolving presence suggests new ways of thinking about transnational boundaries, bodies, ideologies, power structures, medical practices, and late capitalist, Internet-based interactions. Thailand's association with sex-workers is now accompanied by Thailand as a destination for medical work on one's sex, sexuality, sexual functioning, or sexual desirability. The connections proliferate.[71]

Rice, not just stereotypes

I hope that this study functions to further complicate what Thailand *is*. When the individuals and small groups are rendered as complex, historically situated, and creators of their circumstances, Bangkok can be rendered not only the largest Thai city, but also a city with many discrete occupants that play varying roles and respond to particular pressures that are in dialogue with each other, contemporary Thai circumstances, western ideas, economies, and media. The people in this study are agents in our current understanding of sex and gender in Thailand. Their explanations show their strategic deployment of stereotypes in the English language to resituate them in Bangkok and beyond. Put simply, *Import/Export* reveals the complexity of three specific

---

71 Oprah did a special on cosmetic surgery to Thailand featuring a botched eye surgery and a negative review.

sets of people in Thailand in order to show that the use of English marks not only western literacy, but also a strategic grasp of contemporary circumstances.

By exploring these three Bangkok-based communities as well as charting the online changes in Thai tourist packages marketed in English at the beginning of this chapter, the preceding pages underscore the following:

1. Ideas about sex and gender are not the same everywhere. Identical words carry different meanings specific to their time and location.

2. People, whether Thais in Bangkok or westerners thinking about Thailand, have different circumstances and need different tools to make themselves legible both within and beyond their borders and boundaries. The Thai people in my study recognize the specificities of their location—physically and historically. Their strategic use of language enables them to render themselves legible, affect change, and speak on behalf of their small communities to a larger audience, whether locally (to other people in *Anjaree*), cross-culturally (to international NGOs), transnationally (to worldwide gay communities), or globally (through digitally-mediated communication and Internet-based tourism).

Deploying English and actively promoting a multitude of images of Thailand through a variety of media has successfully dislodged historical stereotypes. While generalizations of Thailand and Thai people persist, other, seemingly contradictory, ideas about fine cuisine, upscale vacations, and the pervasive use of high technology coexist. These unequal images side by side mark a disruption from the simplistic, pernicious, and historical western stereotype of a nation replete with compliant, sexually available women and children.

Yet these uses of English are strategic. Each of these groups employ different tactics—claiming the language *tout court* in the case of women-centered NGOs, through negation as in the case of *Anjaree*, or through the use of single terms such as "gay" to name or depict discrete circumstances. With the influx of English, it would be easy to presume that English was merely used as English, not changed based on local needs. Noting how stereotypes flourish and change reveals much about what might be considered fixed or timeless.

For Thais, rice functions as an icon—predetermined and fixed in nutritional, religious, socio-economic and cultural meaning. Until the turn of the century, seventy percent of all Thai people had family members that were rice farmers. Rice is intricately linked to Thai bodies both through the labor involved in its harvesting and as the central form of nourishment. Rice farming is the primary Thai occupation and rice, linguistically, means food. To eat, in Thai, is not simply the word "eat;" to eat is *gin khao*—"eat rice." Similarly, "Are you hungry?" in Thai is *Hue khao mai?*—"Do [you] desire rice? Thai etiquette demands that every grain of rice be consumed as a sign of respect to farmers, culture, and the status of rice—since it is, in essence, nourishment, it must not be wasted. "Are you hungry?"—*Hue khao mai?* does not actually contain a personal pronoun—"you" is implicit when asking the question. The unspoken presumption of "you," of people, is similarly mirrored in the idea that rice is both food and people.[72]

Thais learn that rice and people are intricately connected through sustenance and labor. In all elementary schools in Thailand, children are taught a prayer of gratitude for rice and rice farmers. Elementary school students recite the prayer to rice before eating. The national elementary curriculum requires that teachers explain to young students the value and usefulness of rice. Every Thai elementary student must plant and harvest a grain of rice. In recognition of the rice farmer's labor, each student must transplant rice seedlings. Thai students memorize poetry written by former kings that are odes to rice and the cuisine that surrounds. Rice serves not only as a staple of Thai work and diet, but also as a central image for Thai-derived allegories, clichés, and life lessons.

During my first year in Thailand, as a teacher at a small college, I shared daily lunches with my students in the college cafeteria. After the first month of eating together, students began to quietly rearrange my

---

72 Allusions to rice are much more extensive than I have explained in this brief discussion. For example, when Thais greet each other, they do so by asking not "how are you?" but, "Have [you] eaten rice?" (the you is, as explained above, implied):*Gin khao ma leaw yang?* When referring to prosperity, Thais say: "Have fish in the river and rice in the field" (once again, the "we" is implied, not stated directly): *Me khao nai na, me bla nai num.* Because Thailand is an agriculture land and when they talk about their country and its rich agricultural resources, they say *Nai num me pha, nai na me khao.* ("We have fish in the water, have rice in the field." This suggests that Thai people do not live in poverty because there is food everywhere in the nation. Nationally, imagery suggests wealth through rice and an accompaniment: both fish and rice are ubiquitous to all but the Bangkok urban landscape. When Thais greet each other, they say: *Gin khao ma leaw yong?* "Have you had rice yet?" instead of "How are you?" Supaporn Yavajunawat writes: "We used to worship rice too. We do not throw away rice and step on rice. It is sin." (Personal Correspondence, 2012).

leftover food once it was clear I was finished eating. Each day, one student would quietly take my spoon and fork and gather all the leftover grains of rice on my plate together, forming a small pile. The rest of the food on my plate was untouched. When I asked why different students did the same thing to my plate after each meal together, the students explained that rice is like people—each grain does not want to be left alone. This tale was repeated to me many times during my years in Thailand. Grains of rice and people do not want to be alone. While at odds with the tenets taken for granted from a western humanist perspective that presupposes the primacy of the individual subject and celebrates individualism, people as a group is part and parcel of the Thai understanding of self through their position via the family, their community, their religion, nation, and king.

The meanings attached to rice reveal fundamental differences of worldview and subjectivity between Thai and western culture. Of course myriad differences mark Thai values from not only the U.S. and Europe, but also from the formerly colonized neighboring countries. In Thailand, a kingdom with the longest reigning monarch in history, state and religion are so intertwined that Thais believe their King to be an incarnation of the Buddha. Church and state comprise one another like a tapestry. Similarly, cutting-edge technology is integrated into the lives of the farmers and women weavers captured on the covers of NGO publications discussed in the last chapter. Feature-laden, designer cellphones produced by Nokia are available to Thai consumers, but certain models and designs never appear in the stores of the European company's home. While rural villagers may own cellphones with features more advanced than those marketed to U.S. and European consumers, many still live in homes that lack indoor plumbing,.

The essential Thai national characters of morality as evidenced through rice and religion, both of which illustrate the primacy of interpersonal connections, are eclipsed by western interpretations and globalized media stories. Thailand is sensational rather than complicated; stories about Thailand are tailored to capture, not confuse, western assumptions. More sensational, morally judgmental stereotypes have eclipsed the complex stories about Thai rice-views and proliferate about Thailand beyond its borders.

Childish Renderings

My young daughters have watched me write this book and have wondered why it takes so many pages and countless words to describe a concept they feel competent to capture through drawings. These two images are drawings done several months apart that interpret what each daughter believes this book to explain. Although they have not yet been to Thailand, my daughters are familiar with Thai cultural practices, etiquette, food, and some language through their contact with Thai friends in Chicago. Their understanding of *Import/Export,* may serve to succinctly illustrate the overall points of this study.

Image 5.4

The first image, "Frum Chacogo to Tieland," by Marlena Enteen at age six, shows two almost identical scenes separated by a line. The right side is "Chacago" and the left, "Tieland." On each side of the Chicago/Thailand divide, two stick figures wearing skirts with long hair approach other stick figures, also wearing skirts, with short hair. She says all four figures are girls. On the edge of each scene, framing the stick figures, are two trees. In Chicago, the tree is rounded on top, with leaves. In Thailand the tree has green pointed foliage, palm trees. The palm tree in Thailand has five brown coconuts. For Marlena, the geographical difference is located in the different trees, coconuts, and flower.

In Chicago, the girls approach each other with outstretched hands, and a flower grows between them. In the Thai scene, the two girls walk toward each other with gifts—a coconut and a carrot. My six-year-old daughter imagines these girls looking physically the same in both locations. The cultural interaction is what she has marked as different. When the girls approach each other in Chicago, they have a flower to mark the place where they will meet. In Thailand, their outstretched hands bear gifts. Marlena knows Thailand is tropical and Chicago has flowers. More importantly, she recognizes that Chicago meetings do not include the exchange of gifts. Marlena not only recognizes the cultural specificity of gift exchange in her drawing, she depicts the giving and receiving of food. While she has received many non-edible gifts from Thai people she knows, Marlena inherently understands the importance of food to Thai people and imagines that mutual gift exchange would likely be Thai cuisine, with rice.

Importantly, language marks the other significant difference of this diptych-like rendering. In Chicago, the girl on the left says to the girl she approaches, "Tomboy," and in land-of-coconuts, the little figure with long hair dubs the girl she approaches, "Tom." Both figures use English-language terms, and both the enunciator and the person hailed look similar, but the language use marks the specific terminology appropriate to each location. Vocabulary marks place and meaning, but no fixed meanings are given to these terms. Geography and language are signaled as non-mimetic; each scene depicts cultural, geographical, and linguistic differences that concisely define the adaptation and redeployment of an English-language word. The two corresponding words uttered on both sides of the divide are significantly non-punitive based on Marlena's images. While "tomboy" and "tom" clearly mark gender through short hair, and perhaps sexuality as two girls are depicted as about to embrace, what is foregrounded in both scenes is mutual happiness at seeing each other (smiles), caring (outstretched arms), generosity (flowers, gifts, naming).

by Aaliya Enteen

Image 5.5

The second drawing, by Aaliya Enteen at age seven, is inspired, she explained, by the book's title, *Import/Export*. Aaliya's image, a Venn diagram, is not from a skill set she has learned in school. Instead, she created this set diagram to make a circle not simply a circle. In the imagery that surrounds her, circles represent the earth, the moon, or the sun. Aaliya has already complicated the idea of a simple circle in her artistic rendition of this topic. She complicates her circle in order to reveal that what might be most easily seen as a clear, circle-bound concept, may not, in fact, be so easily outlined. She maintains that this idea seems simple by labeling one circle "Thailand" and the intersecting complement "USA." Thailand's yellow background and USA's blue background each contain paired gendered/sexed outlined images—like those rendered on restrooms doors. The images on both sides are strikingly similar, a corresponding couple. Each couple suggests a gender/sex. On the left is a thick stick figure with no distinguishing marks, and on the right is another with the pointed ends of a skirt. Her drawing suggests that what may look the same may not, in fact, be the same. The intersection of these corresponding circles blends the yellow and blue into green. While the overlapping green area occupies most of the space of Aaliya's image, this space has no gendered/sexed images inside. Thus the large intersection she depicts suggests similarity—and there is more space of overlap than that of difference. While the world could be one, it is not rendered as such in this drawing. And while there is much that is connected, both the distinctly Thai side as well as the USA side are where the mutually exclusive, if almost identical, gendered figures are placed.

Similarity is not simple, and neither culture dominates the other. The intersection—two combined colors—means that mixture certainly happens. However, for Aaliya, it is not the USA that is defining Thailand or vice versa. Each culture occupies distinct space beyond their connection, and the juncture itself is marked by mixture, not U.S. dominance. For Aaliya, *Import/Export* signals a mutual dialogue. She imagines hybridization rather than imperialism; each country and its people are depicted as equally able to navigate, occupy space, and negotiate separate spheres in her world.[73] Aaliya's figures do not inhabit

73 See Homi Bhabha for the invocation of this biological term to cultural

the space of merging culture. Rather, each set of people has access to the largest space of intersection. While it may initially seem as if Thailand "imports" sexed/gendered terms more than it "exports," Aaliya depicts cultural crossings as accessible, not gated. Her equal figures stand on the outskirts with the suggestion of equality and mutuality, yet also the potential to remain discrete in addition to large spaces of overlap.

What to Conclude?

As the children's illustrations take for granted, similar appearances do not presume identical interpretation. There are no absolutes about what gender might mean, yet both drawings are premised on the notion that things are most likely not identical despite initial visual similarity. These drawings render with ease the idea that no essential, timeless, non-specific gender or sexuality can or should be presumed. Likewise, neither daughter presumes to reveal truths about sex or gender in Thailand. Instead what is evident is that conceptions of sex and gender are constantly in flux, responding to historical pressures and contemporary circumstances. The interviews of the specific Bangkok groups in the previous chapters clarify that "natural" sex and gender in Thailand is not necessarily the same "natural" as we know it in the west. Accordingly, "natural" is not something inherent or ever-present or permanent. Instead, it is an act of making meaning that changes across groups of people.

The information in this book suggests that one can read for knowledge, not for truth. Logics make sense all around the world—

intersections.

situation, context, and relativity are all factors that change someone's life. Without ethnography, we can't understand the knowledge we are acquiring. If we don't understand the situation, we might simply take the knowledge as a stereotype. If we understand one situation, it opens the door to understanding and imagining multiple situations/contexts, so that we are pushed to critically think about our assumptions in our own personal situation. If "knowledge" is simply consolidated, vetted, and nuanced stereotypes, we must recognized that there are always caveats in what we read—even in prestigious academic journals. Other cultures consisting of millions of people understand and act according to assumptions different than our own, from the seemingly straightforward function of rice to what constitutes male, female, gay, masculine, or feminine. When we understand that many people operate with constraints as equally fixed as our own, then we are able to stretch our thinking beyond our own cultural truisms to reexamine our cultural contexts, question our presumptions of truth, and use language and communication to better describe the myriad ways in which gender and sex might be articulated in each specific iteration.

Reading about far-flung places is interesting. Debunking the persistent stereotypes about Thailand is potentially powerful. Thinking about sex and gender is fascinating as it's an easy commonality that is central to the western imagination. The information presented in the previous pages about these specific groups in Bangkok might suggest that what's imported, exported, natural, and normal to one person is illegible to other groups. Assumptions and stereotypes are generated, reified, dislodged, or pernicious. Decentering enduring generalizations is occurring, but truth or evidence has little to do with their existence. The earlier chapters have provided a glimpse of a very small, but very complicated terrain that collects new members and, each day, creates new histories of the conditions of sex and gender in contemporary Bangkok.

I hope that what began as a small survey, like a tourist visit to Thailand, has revealed far more than facts about the use of English-language terms for sex and gender. Certainly this knowledge about Thailand, sex, gender, socio-economic transnational conditions, and contemporary transnational politics has increased. Ultimately, however, the challenge you to continue thinking about strategies, stereotypes, and what is fixed, pre-determined, and natural—whether experiencing "Amazing Thailand" or home, wherever that may be.

Bibliography

@TOMact Magazine. http://www.atomact.com. Issue 1, Jan
    2008-Issue 17, Jan 2010. (Annual Mr. Tom voting at http://
    mr.atomact.com/mratom.html.)

Abelove, Henry Michele Aina Barale, and David M. Halperin, eds. *The
    Lesbian and Gay Studies Reader*. New York: Routledge, 1993.

Adventurous Traveler Bookstore. Online. Internet. 11 Apr. 1995. shop.
    gorp.com/atbook/bookloc.asp?location_id_WRD.

Allyn, E. G., ed. *The Dove Coos: Gay Experiences by The Men of
    Thailand*. Trans. Nukul Benchamat and Somboon Inpradith.
    Bangkok: Bua Luang Publishing, 1992. -

--. The *Men of Thailand Guide to Thailand*. Ed. Samorn Chaiyana.
    5thed. Bangkok: Floating Lotus Press, 1995.

Alonso, Ana Maria and Maria Teresa Koreck. "Silences: 'Hispanics,'
    AIDS, and Sexual Practices." *Lesbian and Gay Studies Reader*.
    Ed. Henry Abelove, Michele Aina Barale, and David M.
    Halperin. New York: Routledge, 1993. 110-126.

alt.sex.prostitution. Online. Usenet.

Altman, Dennis. "Global Gaze/Global Gays." *GLQ: A Journal of
    Lesbian and Gay Studies* 3.4 (1997): 417-436.

---. *Global Sex.* Chicago: University of Chicago Press, 2001.

---. "Rupture or Continuity? The Internationalization of Gay Identities." *Social Text* 48 (Fall 1996): 77-94.

Anderson, Benedict R. *Imagined Communities: Reflections on the Origin and Spread of Nationalism.* London: Verso, 1983.

---. *The Spectre of Comparisons: Nationalism, Southeast Asian and the World.* New York: Verso, 1998.

---. "Studies of the Thai State: The State of Thai Studies." *The Study of Thailand: Analyses of*

Knowledge, Approaches, and Prospects in Anthropology, Art History, Economics,

History and Political Science. Ed. Eliezer B. Ayal. Ohio: Ohio University Center for International Studies, 1978.

---. Personal Correspondence. June 1997.

Anderson, Benedict and Ruchira Mendiones, *In the Mirror: Politics in Siam in the American Era.* Southeast Asia Program Publications, 1985.

Anjaree official website. http://anjaree.org/11001.html

Ann (Name changed). Personal Interview. 18 October 1996.

Appadurai, Arjun. *Modernity at Large: Cultural Dimensions of Globalization.* Minneapolis:

University of Minnesota Press, 1997.

---. "Disjuncture and Difference in the Global Cultural Economy."
Public Culture 2.2 (1990): 1-24.

Aribarg, Suwatana. "Seen Through the Eyes of Thai Parents." *Bangkok Post* 21 June 95: 31.

Bakhtin, Mikhail M. *The Dialogic Imagination: Four Essays*. Ed. M. Holquist. Trans. C.

Emerson and M. Holquist. Austin: Texas University Press, 1981.

Balibar, Etienne. "The Nation Form: History and Ideology." *Race, Nation, Class: Ambiguous*

Identities. Ed. Etienne Balibar and Immanuel Wallerstein. New York: Verso, 1992. 86-106.

Barme, Scot. "Luang Wichit Wathakan and the Creation of a Thai Identity." *New Studies of Nationalism*. Ed. Eric Hobsbawn, Ben Anderson and Liah Greenfield. Singapore: Institute for Southeast Asian Studies, 1993. 226-243.

Barnet, Richard J. and John Cavanagh. *Global Dreams: Imperial Corporations and the New World Order*." New York: Simon and Schuster, 1994.

Bhaopichitr, Kirida. "Thailand's Road to Economic Crisis: A Brief Overview." *Nation*. Online.

Internet. 18 Dec. 1997. www.nationmultimedia.com.

Bishop, Ryan and Lillian S. Robinson. *Night Market: Sexual Cultures and the Thai Economic Miracle*. New York: Routledge, 1998.

Blank, Grant. "The Road Ahead: Observations on the Role of the Internet." *Social Science Computer Review* 15.2 (Summer 1997): 190-195.

Bliss, Jennifer and Crab Boy. "Butch Among the Straights: Crab Boy with Jennifer Bliss." *Pink Ink: Thailand's Gay and Lesbian Monthly*. 1.2 (November 1997): 6. Also located at http://www.khsnet. com/pinkink/vol1-2/butch.htm.

---. "International Pink Briefing." *Pink Ink: Thailand's Gay and Lesbian Monthly*. 1.3 (December 1997): 1.

---. "Braving Worlds of Disapproval: Crab Boy with Jennifer Bliss." *Pink Ink: Thailand's Gay and Lesbian Monthly*. 1.3 (December 1997): 8. Also located at http://www.khsnet.com/pinkink/vol1-3/ crabboy.htm.

---. "Major Boost for Lesbian Rights." *Pink Ink: Thailand's Gay and Lesbian Monthly*.1.4 (January 1998). Online. http://www. khsnet.com/pinkink/vol1-4/lead1.htm

---. "Lesbofile." *Pink Ink: Thailand's Gay and Lesbian Monthly*. 1.4 (January 1998). Online. Internet. http://www.khsnet.com/ pinkink/vol1-4/crabboy.htm.

Blunt, Alison and Gillian Rose, ed. *Writing Women and Space: Colonial and PostcolonialGeographies*. New York: Guilford Press, 1994.

Boonchalaksi, W. and Philip Guest. *Prostitution in Thailand*. IPSR Publication No. 171. Nakhon Pathom: Institute for Population and Social Research, Mahidol University, 1994.

"The Boy Who Grew Up into a Woman." *Bangkok Post* 15 Apr. 96: 24. Boykin, Keith. *One More River to Cross: Black and Gay in America*. New York: Anchor Books, 1996.

Bruckman, Amy S. "Gender Swapping on the Internet." *High Noon on the Electric Frontier*. Ed. Peter Ludlow. Cambridge: MIT Press, 1996: 317-325.

Busia, Abena and Stanlie James, eds. *Theorizing Black Feminisms*. New York: Routledge, 1993.

Butler, Judith. *Bodies that Matter: On the Discursive Limits of "Sex."* New York: Routledge, 1993.

---. *Gender Trouble: Feminism and the Subversion of Identity*. New York: Routledge, 1990.

Callahan, William. "Sister Number One: the Television Production of Miss Thailand in State, Consumer and Transnational Space." Unpublished article. Bangkok, 1993.

Carol (Name Changed). Personal Interview. 10 May 1996.

Carter, Erica, et al. *Space and Place: Theories of Identity and Location*. London: Lawrence and Wishart, 1993.

Case, Sue Ellen. "Toward a Butch-Femme Aesthetic." *Lesbian and Gay Studies Reader*. Ed. Henry Abelove, Michele Aina Barale, and

David M. Halperin. New York: Routledge, 1993. 294-306.

Chakravarty, Pratap. "Eunuch Enters Fray in India General Election." *Nation* 7 May 96: A11.

Chamsanit, Varaporn. "A Plea for Tolerance." *Nation* 28 Feb. 96: C3.

---. Personal Interviews. Conducted between March 96 and April 98.

Chatterjee, Partha. *The Nation and Its Fragments: Colonial and Postcolonial Histories*. Princeton: Princeton University Press, 1998.

Chauncey, George. *Gay New York: Gender, Urban Culture, and the Making of the Gay World 1890-1940*. New York: Basic Books, 1994.

Cheah, Pheng and Bruce Robbins, eds. *Cosmopolitics: Thinking and Feeling beyond the Nation*. Minneapolis: University of Minnesota Press, 1998.

Cheesman, Patricia. *Lao Textiles: Ancient Symbols--Living Art*. Bangkok: White Lotus Press, 1988. 126-148.

Chiwit Nai Chat (*Life in the Nation*). Bangkok, n.d.

Chow, Rey. *Ethics after Idealism: Theory--Culture--Ethnicity--Reading*. Bloomington: Indiana University Press, 1998.

Chowdhry, Geeta. "Engendering Development? Women in Development (WID) in International Development Regimes." *Feminism/Postmodernism/Development*. Ed. Marchand and

Parpart. New York: Routledge, 1995.

Chutikul, Saisuree. Personal Interview. 11 Sept. 1995.

Cohen, Lawrence. "Holi in Bananara and the Mahaland of Modernity." *GLQ: A Journal of Lesbian and Gay Studies* 4.2 (1998): 399-424.

Collot, Milena and Nancy Belmore. "Electronic Language: A new variety of English." *Computer-Mediated Communication: Linguistic, Social and Cross-Cultural Perspectives*. Ed. Susan C. Herring. Philadelphia: John Benjamins Publishing Company, 1996. 13-28.

Cornwel-Smith, Philip and John Goss. *Very Thai: Everyday Popular Culture*. Bangkok: River Books, 2004.

---. *Very Thai 2: Everyday Popular Culture*. Bangkok: River Books, 2013.

Cook, Nerida. "Thailand: 'Dutiful Daughters,' Estranged Sisters." *Gender and Power in Affluent Asia*. Ed. Krishna Sen and Maila Stivens. New York: Routledge, 1998. 250-90.

Cooper, Robert and Nanthapa. *Culture Shock!: Thailand*. 2nd ed. Portland, Oregon: Graphic Arts Center Publishing Company, 1990.

Cornwall, Richard R. "Queer Political Economy: The Social Articulation of Desire." *Homo Economics: Capitalism, Community, and Lesbian and Gay Life*. Ed. Amy Gluckman and

Betsy Reed. New York: Routledge, 1997. 89-122.

De Lauretis, Teresa. *Technologies of Gender: Essays on Theory, Film, and Fiction*. Bloomington: Indiana University Press, 1987.

Diderich, Joelle. "Hit Films Woo Mainstream Public to London's Drag Clubs." *Nation* 3 Nov. 95: C3.

"Disc Jockeys Charged with Procuring Boys." *Nation* 18 Oct. 95: D3.

Dollimore, Jonathan. *Sexual Dissidence: Augustine to Wilde, Freud to Foucault*. New York: Oxford, 1991.

Eldridge, Philip J. *Non-Government Organizations and Democratic Participation in Indonesia*. New York: Oxford University Press, 1995.

---. "Non-Government Organizations, the State, and Democratization in Indonesia." *Imagining Indonesia: Cultural Politics and Political Culture*. Ed. Jim Schiller and Barbara Martin   Schiller. Ohio: Center for International Studies, 1997.

EMPOWER foundation. Last updated November 2012. http://www. empowerfoundation.org/sexy_en.php#.

Enteen, Jillana. "Northwest WorldPerks: Speaking about the Hmong Diaspora from the Orientalist/Western Feminist Paradigm." "Diasporas Old and New" Conference. New Brunswick, March 1994.

---. *Virtual English: Queer Internets and Digital Creolization*. New York: Routledge, 2010.

Featherstone, Mike, ed. *Global Culture: Nationalism, Globalization and Modernity*. Newbury   Park, CA: Sage Publications, 1990.

---. Scott Lash and Roland Robertson, eds. *Global Modernities*. London: Sage Publications, 1995.

Fisher, Julie. *Nongovernments: NGOs and the Political Development of the Third World*. West Hartford, Connecticut: Kumarian Press, 1998.

Foucault, Michel. *The History of Sexuality, Volume 1: An Introduction*. Trans. Robert Hurley. New York: Vintage, 1980.

Friedman, Thomas L. "The Thai Bind." *New York Times* 11 Dec. 1997: A27.

Friends of Women Newsletter. Bangkok: Friends of Women Foundation.

Fon (Name Changed). Personal Interview. 19 March 1996.

Fung, Richard. "Looking for My Penis: The Eroticized Asian in Gay Video Porn." *How Do I Look?: Queer Film and Video*. Ed. Bad Object-Choices. Seattle: Gay Press, 1991. 145-168.

Fuss, Diana. *Essentially Speaking: Feminism, Nature and Difference*. New York: Routledge, 1990.

Ghosh, Chitra. *The World of Thai Women*. Calcutta: Best Books, 1990.

Gikandi, Simon E. "The Postcolonial Inheritance: Reading the Ruins of Modernity." MLA Convention. Toronto. 28 Dec. 1997.

Goldberg, Jonathan. *Queering the Renaissance*. Durham: Duke University Press, 1993. Gouveia, Georgette. "Hollywood Stars Stay in the Closet." *Nation* 3 Nov. 95: C3.

---. "The Gay Revolution." *Nation* 3 Nov. 95: C3.

Gupta, Akhil and James Ferguson. "Beyond 'Culture': Space, Identity and the Politics of Dislocation." *Cultural Anthropology* 7.1 (February 1992): 6-23.

GWG Newsletter. Bangkok: Gender and Development Research Institute.

Halberstam, Judith. *Female Masculinities*. Durham: Duke University Press, 1998.

---. "Mackdaddy, Superfly, Rapper: Gender, Race and Masculinity in the Drag King Scene." *Social Text* 15.3/4 (1997): 104-132.

Hall, Kira. "Cyberfeminism." *Computer-Mediated Communication: Linguistic, Social and   Cross-Cultural Perspectives*. Ed. Susan C. Herring. Philadelphia: John Benjamins   Publishing Company, 1996. 147-170.

Haraway, Donna. *Simians, Cyborgs and Women: The Reinvention of Nature*. New York: Routledge, 1991.

Harper, Phillip Brian, Anne McClintock, Jose Esteban Munoz and Trish Rosen. "Queer   Transexions of Race, Nation, and Gender: An Introduction." *Social Text* 15.3/4   (1997): 1-4.

Herdt, Gilbert, ed. *Third Sex Third Gender: Beyond Sexual Dimorphism in Culture and History*. New York: Zone Books, 1994.

Herring, Susan C., ed. *Computer-Mediated Communication: Linguistic, Social and CrossCultural Perspectives*. Philadelphia: John Benjamins Publishing Company, 1996.

Huntington, Samuel P. *The Clash of Civilizations and the Remaking of World Order*. New   York: Simon and Schuster, 1996.

Jackson, Peter. *Dear Uncle Go: Male Homosexuality in Thailand*. Bangkok: Bua Luang   Publishing, 1995.

---, Ed. *Queer Bangkok : twenty-first-century markets, media, and rights* Chiang Mai, Thailand: Silkworm Books, 2011.

--- and Gerard Sullivan, Eds. Lady Boys, Tom Boys, Rent Boys: Male and Female

Homosexualities in Contemporary Thailand. New York: Harrington Park   Press, 1999.

Jameson, Fredric. "Notes on Globalization as a Philosophical Issue." *Cultures of Globalization*. Ed. Fredric Jameson and Masao Miyoshi. Durham: Duke University Press, 1998. 54-77.

---. "Postmodernism, of the Cultural Logic of Late Capitalism." *New Left Review* 146 (July   August 1984): 53-92.

--- and Masao Miyoshi, eds. *Cultures of Globalization*. Durham: Duke University Press,1998.

Jayawardena, Kumari. *Feminism and Nationalism in the Third World*.

London: Zed Books, 1986.

Joe (Name Changed). Personal interviews. Conducted between Aug. 1995 and Jan. 1998.

---. Written thoughts. May 1996.

Jones, Steven G., ed. *Virtual Culture: Identity and Communication in Cybersociety*. London: Sage Publications, 1997.

Jusdanus, Gregory. "Culture, Culture Everywhere: The Swell of Globalization Theory." *Diaspora*   5.1 (1996): 128-145.

Jussawalla, Meheroo, ed. *Telecommunications: A Bridge to the 21st Century*. New York: North   Holland, 1995.

Kahn, Joseph. "Folk Hero Strips Teflon from Thailand's Corrupt." *New York Times* 26 Apr. 98: 3.

---. "Was That a Lady I Saw You Boxing?" *New York Times* 4 Apr. 98: A4.

Kanjanawanawan, Suda. "Crossing the Gender Divide." *Bangkok Post* 12 Aug. 95: 31.

Kaplan, Caren. "'Getting to Know You': Travel, Gender, and the Politics of Representation in *Anna and the King of Siam* and *The King and I*." *Late Imperial Culture*. Ed. Roman   de la Campa, E. Ann Kaplan, and Michael Sprinker. New York: Verso, 1995. 33-52.

Katz, Jonathan. *Gay American History: Lesbians and Gay Men in the U.S.A.* New York: Crowell, 1976.

Keith, Michael and Steve Pile, eds. *Place and the Politics of Identity*.
New York: Routledge, 1993.

Klausner, William J. *Reflections on Thai Culture*. Bangkok: The Siam
Society Under Royal   Patronage, 1993

Korenman, Joan and Nancy Wyatt. "Group Dynamics in an e-mail
Forum." *Computer   Mediated Communication: Linguistic,
Social and Cross-Cultural Perspectives*. Ed.   Susan C.
Herring. Philadelphia: John Benjamins Publishing Company,
1996. 225-242.

Koshy, Susan. "From Cold War to Trade War: Neocolonialism and
Human Rights." *Social Text* 58 (Spring 1999) 1-32.

Kriengkraipetch, Suvanna and Larry E. Smith. *Value Conflicts in Thai
Society: Agonies of Change Seen in Short Stories*. Bangkok: Social
Research Institute of Chulalongkorn University, 1992.

Kulick, Don. *Travesti: Sex, Gender and Culture among Brazilian
Transgendered Prostitutes*. Chicago: University of Chicago Press,
1998.

Laplamvanit, Narisa. "A Little of Fortune." Online. Internet. www.
columbia.edu/cu/thai/html/tsa_women.html.

Law (Name changed). Personal Interviews. Aug. 1995- May 1996.

Lek (Name changed). Personal Interview. 13 May 1996.

Lerdsrisuntad, Usa. Personal Interview. 30 May 1996.

Linton, Malcolm. "The Boys Who Steal the Show." *Bangkok Post* 2 Aug. 1992: 27+.

Loos, Tamara Lynn. *Subject Siam : family, law, and colonial modernity in Thailand*. Ithaca: Cornell University Press, 2006.

Ma, Ringo. "Computer-Mediated Conversations as a New Dimension of Intercultural Communication between East Asian and North American College Students." *Computer Mediated Communication: Linguistic, Social and Cross-Cultural Perspectives*. Ed. Susan C. Herring. Philadelphia: John Benjamins Publishing Company, 1996. 173-185.

Manalanson IV, Martin F. "(Dis)Orienting the Body: Locating Symbolic Resistance among Filipino Gay Men." *Positions* 2:1 (1994): 73-90.

Mardon, Russell, and Won K. Paik. "The State, Foreign Investment, and Sustaining Industrial Growth in South Korea and Thailand." *The Evolving Pacific Basin in the Global Political Economy: Domestic and International Linkages*. Ed. Cal Clark and Steve Chan. Boulder: Lynne Rienner Publishers, 1992.

Marriott, Michel. "The Web Reflects a Wider World: As More Non-English Speakers Log On, Many Languages Thrive." *New York Times* 18 June 98: G1+.

Masner, Andrew. "Into the Light: The Thai Lesbian Movement Takes a Step Forward." *ISIS International.* (originally in Isis International's *Women in Action* (3) 1998: http://www.isiswomen.org/index.php?option=com_

content&view=article&id=550). http://www.isiswomen.org/ index.php?option=com content&view=article&id=550:into-the-light&catid=133.

Massey, Doreen. *Space, Place, and Gender*. Minneapolis: University of Minnesota Press, 1994.

Maxwell, Robyn. "Traditions Transformed: The Cultural Context of Textile Making and Use in Southeast Asia." *Cultures at Crossroads: Southeast Asian Textiles from the Australian National Gallery*. Ed. Graham Grayston. Sidney: Australian National Gallery, 1992. 11 24.

McClintock, Anne. *Imperial Leather: Race, Gender and Sexuality in the Colonial Contest*. New York: Routledge, 1995.

McLaughlin et al. "Virtual Community in a Telepresence Environment." *Virtual Culture: Identity and Communication in Cybersociety*. Ed. Steven G. Jones. London: Sage Publications, 1997. 10-35.

Meagher, Mary Elaine and Fernando Castanos. "Perceptions of American Culture: The Impact of an Electronically-Mediated Cultural Exchange Program on Mexican High School Students." *Computer-Mediated Communication: Linguistic, Social and Cross-Cultural Perspectives*. Ed. Susan C. Herring. Philadelphia: John Benjamins Publishing Company, 1996. 187-201.

Meo (Name Changed). Personal Communication. 19 September 1996.

Mignolo, Walter D. "Globalization, Civilization Processes, and the Relocation of Languages and Cultures." *Cultures of Globalization*. Ed. Fredric Jameson and Masao Miyoshi. Durham: Duke University Press, 1998. 32-53.

Mishra, Vijay and Bob Hodge. "What is Post(-)colonialism?" *Colonial Discourse and Post Colonial Theory: A Reader*. Ed. Patrick Williams and Laura Chrisman. New York: Columbia University Press, 1994. 276-290.

Mitra, Ananda. "Virtual Commonality: Looking for India on the Internet." *Virtual Culture: Identity and Communication in Cybersociety*. Ed. Steven G. Jones. London: Sage Publications, 1997. 55-79.

Mohanty, Chandra Talpade and M. J. Alexander, eds. *Feminist Geneologies, Colonial Legacies, Democratic Futures*. New York: Routledge, 1996.

---, Ann Russo and Lourdes Torres, eds. *Third World Women and the Politics of Feminism*. Bloomington: Indiana University Press, 1991.

Moraga, Cherrie and Gloria Anzaldua, eds. *This Bridge Called My Back: Writings by Radical Women of Color*. Watertown, Mass: Persephone Press, 1981.

Morris, Rosalind C. "Three Sexes and Four Sexualities: Redressing the Discourses on Gender and Sexuality in Contemporary Thailand." *Positions* 2.1 (1994): 15-43.

---. "Educating Desire: Thailand, Transnationalism, and Transgression." *Social Text* 15.3/4 (1997): 53-79.

National Commission on Women's Affairs. *Thai Women.* Bangkok, Amarindra Printing Group, 1993.

National Information Infrastructure. *The (NII). Agenda for Action, Executive Summary.* Washington, 15 Sept. 1993.

Nestle, Joan, ed. *The Persistent Desire: A Femme-Butch Reader.* Boston: Alyson Publications, 1992.

Oat (Name changed). Personal Interviews. Aug 1995-June 1996, 2004.

Office of the National Human Rights Commission of Thailand. "NHRCT organized a public forum, "The Next Step of Human Rights and LGBTIQ Peoples." Posted 29 November 2012. Accessed 23 March 3012. http://www.nhrc.or.th/2012/wb/en/news_detail.php?nid=1329&parent_id=1&type=hilight.

Paolillo, John C. "Code-switching on the Internet: Panjabi and English on soc.culture.panjab." Georgetown University Round Table on Languages and Linguistics, Presession on Computer-Mediated Discourse Analysis. Mar. 1995.

Pari (Name changed). Personal Interview. 15 Oct. 1996.

Parker, Andrew, et al. *Nationalisms and Sexualities.* New York: Routledge, 1992.

Perry, Michael. "Festival Puts Australia on Gay Tourist Map." *Bangkok Post* 5 Mar. 96: 36.

Phongpaichit, Pasuk. Personal Interview. 25 May 1996.

---. and Chris Baker. *Thai Capital after the 1997 Crisis*. Chiang Mai: Silkworm Press, 2008.

---. *Thailand's Boom!* Chiang Mai, Thailand: Silkworm Press, 1996.

---. *Thailand: Economy and Politics*. Oxford, Oxford University Press, 1995.

Phuket Plastic Surgery Center. Online. Internet. thaibiz.com/phuket-plasticsurgery/index.htm.

Plant, Sadie. "The Future Looms: Weaving Women and Cybernetics." *Clicking In: Hot Links to a Digital Culture*. Ed. Lynn Hershman Leeson. Seattle: Bay Press, 1996. 123-135.

Pongsapich, Amara. "Feminism Theories and Praxi: Women's Social Movement in Thailand." 6th International Conference on Thai Studies. Chiang Mai, 16 Oct. 1996.

---. "Strengthening the Role of NGOs in Popular Participation." *Thai NGOs: The Continuing Struggle for Democracy*. Ed. Jaturong Boonyarattanasoontorn and Gawin Chutima. Bangkok: Thai NGO Support Project, 1995. 9-50.

Pornpitagpan, Nilubol. "Weaving Dreams in the Name of Peace." *Friends of Women Newsletter*   (December 1992): 8.

Porter, David, ed. *Internet Culture*. New York: Routledge, 1997.

Pramoj, Kukrit. *Si Phaendin (Four Reigns)*. Book One. Trans.

Tulachandra. Bangkok: Duang Kamol, n.d. Reprinted Chiang Mai: Silkworm Press, 1999. (Originally published in Thai in 1954.

Promate, Mr. Interview January 2, 2014. Tourism Authority of Thailand , Bangkok Office at 1600 New Phetchaburi Road, Makkasan, Ratchathevi , Bangkok 10400. Translated by Naremon Pratanwanich.

Pui (Name changed). Series of interviews and e-mail correspondence. Jan. 1996 - Dec. 1998.

Rajan, Rajeswari Sunder. *Real and Imagined Women: Gender, Culture and Postcolonialism.* New York: Routledge, 1993.

Rheingold, Howard. *The Virtual Community: Homesteading on the Electronic Frontier.* Reading, MA: Addison-Wesley Publishing Co., 1993.

---. "A Slice of Life in my Virtual Community." *Global Networks: Computers and International Commucation.* Ed L. M. Harasim. Cambridge: MIT Press, 1993. 57-80.

Riding, Alan "When Movie Actors From France Dare to Look to the West." *New York Times* 24 May 98: 11+.

Robertson, Roland. "Glocalization: Time-Space and Homogeneity-Heterogeneity." *Global Modernities.* Ed. Mike Featherstone. London: Sage Publications, 1995. 77-92.

Robbins, Bruce. *Feeling Global: Internationalism in Distress.* New York:

New York University Press, 1999.

Roscoe, Will. "Was We'Wha a Homosexual?: A Native American Survivance and the Two-Spirit Tradition." *GLQ: A Journal of Lesbian and Gay Studies* 2.3 (1995):193-235.

Rose, Jacqueline. "The State of the Subject (1): The Institution of Feminism." *Critical Quarterly* 29.4 (Winter 1987): 9-15.

Sassen, Saskia. "Analytic Borderlands: Race, Gender and Representation in the New City." *Re-presenting the City: Ethnicity, Capital and Culture in the 21st-Century Metropolis*. Ed. Anthony D. King. New York: New York University Press, 1996. 184-206.

Schiller, Herbert I. "The Global Information Highway: Project for an Ungovernable World." *Resisting the Virtual Life: The Culture and Politics of Information*. Ed. James Brook and Iain A. Boal. San Fransisco: City Lights, 1995. 17-33.

Seabrook, Jeremy. *Travels in the Skin Trade: Tourism and the Sex Industry*. Chicago: Pluto Press, 1996.

Segaller, Denis. *Thai Ways*. 3rd ed. Bangkok: Post Books, 1993.

Sen, Krishna and Maila Stivens, eds. *Gender and Power in Affluent Asia*. New York: Routledge, 1998.

Shields, Rob, ed. *Cultures of Internet: Virtual Space, Real Histories, Living Bodies*. Thousand Oaks, Sage Publications, 1996.

Shiva, Vandana. *Staying Alive: Women, Ecology and Development*. New Jersey: Zed Books, 1989.

Shohat, Ella. "The Struggle over Representation: Casting, Coalitions, and the Politics of   Identification." *Late Imperial Culture.* Ed. Roman de la Campa, E. Ann Kaplan, and Michael Sprinker. New York: Verso, 1995. 166-178.

SiamWEB. Online. Internet. www.siamweb.org.

Silver, David. "Book of the Month Review." *RCCS on-line.* Online. Internet.

Simmons, Pam. Personal Interview. 30 May 1996.

Sinnott, Megan. *Toms and Dees: Transgender Identity and Female Same-Sex Relationships in Thailand.* Honolulu : University of Hawaii Press, 2004.

Smith, Emily. "Gender-Bending from Backstage to Limelight." *Bangkok Post* 19 Apr. 96: 32+.

Spivak, Gayatri Chakravorty. *Outside in the Teaching Machine.* New York: Routledge, 1993.

---. *In Other Worlds: Essays in Cultural Politics.* New York: Routledge, 1988.

Stallybrass, Peter and Allon White. *The Politics and Poetics of Transgression.* Ithaca, Cornell University Press, 1986.

Stone, Allucquere Rosanne. "Will the Real Body Please Stand Up? Boundary Stories About Virtual Cultures." *Cyberspace: First Steps.* Ed. Michael Benedikt. Cambridge: MIT,1991. 81-118.

Sullivan, Caitlin and Kate Bornstein. *Nearly Roadkill: An Infobahn Erotic Adventure*. New York: High Risk, 1996.

Susan (Name changed). Personal Interview. 17 May 1996.

Suriyasarn, Busakorn. "Cyberdiscourse on Thai Women on *soc.culture. thai*: A Perspective on Gender Politics on the Internet." Online. Internet. oak.cats.ohiou.edu/~bs388085/cyber qualitative1.htm.

Suvarnananda, Anjana. "Gender Bending." Foreign Correspondents' Club of Thailand, Bangkok. 17 Jan. 1995.

---. "Lesbianism: A Social Problem?" Sixth International Conference of Thai Studies, Chiang Mai, Thailand, 16 Oct. 1996.

---. Personal Interview. Chiang Mai, 16 Oct. 1996.

Taiyo Language School. Online. Internet. www.geocities.com/Athens/ Olympus/9145.

Tantiwiramanond, Darunee and Shashi Ranjan Pandey. *By Women, For Women: A Study of Women's Organizations in Thailand*. Social Issues in Southeast Asia, Research Notes and   Discussions Paper No. 72. Singapore: Institute of Southeast Asian Studies, 1991.

---. "New Opportunities or New Inequalities: Development Issues and Women's Lives in Thailand." *Proceedings of the Sixth International Conference on Thai Studies, Theme 5: Women, Gender Relations and Development in Thai Society*. Chiang Mai: 1996. 79-110.

"Thai Lesbian Rights Group Protests SCT." *Nation* 12 Feb. 96: A1+.

Thai Women. Bangkok: National Commission on Women's Affairs, 1992.

Thailand's Got Talent. Mr. Tom 2013. 30 June 2013. https://www. youtube.com/watch?v=2SQ0iieAqQU. Published 25 July 2013. Accessed 28 August 2014.

Thailand in the 90s. Rev. Ed. Bangkok: National Identity Office of the Prime Minister, 1995.

Thailand Med Tourism: The Thailand Medical Tourist Portal. Promoted by the Tourist Authoirty of Thailand. Bangkok, Thailand. Online. Internet. http://www.thailandmedtourism.com/ Home/28. Accessed 21 March 2014.

Thomson, Suteera. Personal Interview. 12 Oct. 1995.

---. and Maytinee Bhongsvej. *Profile of Women in Thailand*. Bangkok: Gender and Development Research Institute, 1995.

Thongthiraj, Took Took. "Toward a Struggle against Invisibility: Love Between Women in Thailand." *Amerasia Journal* 20.1 (1994): 45-58.

Tourism Authority of Thailand. Online. Internet. www.inet.co.th/ org/tncwa/Early.htm. Accessed 1996. Site changed in 19980: http://www.tourismthailand.org.

Trinh, T. Minh-ha. *Woman, Native, Other: Writing Postcoloniality and Feminism*. Bloomington: Indiana University Press, 1989.

Tuathail, Gearoid O. and Simon Dalby. "Rethinking Geopolitics: Towards a Critical Geopolitics." *Rethinking Geopolitics*. Gearoid O Tuathail and Simon Dalby, eds. New   York: Routledge, 1998. 1-15.

Turkle, Sherry. *Life on the Screen: Identity in the Age of the Internet*. New York: Simon and Schuster, 1995.

van Wijngaarden, Jan W. de Lind. "A Social Geography of Male Homosexual Desire: An Exploration of Locations, Individuals, Groups and Networks in the Context of the   HIV/ AIDS Epidemic in Northern Thailand." Sixth International Conference of Thai Studies, Chiang Mai, Thailand. 15 Oct. 1996.

Voices of Thai Women. Bangkok: Foundation for Women.

Wall, Cheryl, ed. *Changing our Own Words: Essays on Criticism, Theory, and Writing by Black Women*. New Brunswick: Rutgers, 1991.

Watson, Nessim. "Why We Argue About Virtual Community: A Case Study of the Phish.Net Fan Community." *Virtual Culture: Identity and Communication in Cybersociety*. Ed. Steven G. Jones. London: Sage Publications, 1997. 102-132.

"Weaving New Life Project, The "*Voices of Thai Women*" 11 (July 1994): cover image, 12.

Weeks, Jeffrey. *Invented Moralities: Sexual Values in an Age of Uncertainty*. New York: Columbia University Press, 1995.

Weiss, Thomas G. and Leon Gordenker, eds. *NGOs, the UN, and Global Governance*. Boulder,   Colorado: Lynne Rienner Publishers, Inc., 1996.

Werry, Christopher. "Linguistic and Interactional Features of Internet Relay Chat." *Computer Mediated Communication: Linguistic, Social and Cross-Cultural Perspectives*. Ed. Susan   C. Herring. Philadelphia: John Benjamins Publishing Company, 1996. 46-63.

"When Little Girls are Made of Boys." *Nation* 10 Mar. 96: C10.

Wilford, Rick and Robert L. Miller, eds. *Women, Ethnicity and Nationalism: The Politics of Transition*. New York: Routledge, 1998.

Wilson, Ara. The Intimate Economies of Bangkok: Tomboys, Tycoons, and Avon Ladies in the Global City. Berkeley: University of California Press, 2004.

Wilson, Donald and David Henley. "Portrait of a Paedophile." *Bangkok Post* 3 Mar. 96: 19+.

Winichakul, Thongchai. *Siam Mapped: A History of the Geo-body of a Nation*. Chiang Mai: Silkworm Press, 1994.

Wise, J. Macgregor. *Exploring Technology and Social Space*. Thousand Oaks: Sage, 1997.

World Sex Guide. Online. Internet. www.paranoia.com/faq/prostitution.

Wyatt, David K. *Thailand: A Short History*. 2nd ed. New Haven: Yale

University Press, 1984.

Ziv, Oren. "Writing to Work: How Using e-mail can Reflect Technological and Organizational Change." *Computer-Mediated Communication: Linguistic, Social and Cross-Cultural Perspectives*. Ed. Susan C. Herring. Philadelphia: John Benjamins Publishing Company, 1996. 243-264.

Index